Paul Ferrini's work is a must read
take responsibility for their own healing.

JOHN BRADSHAW

Paul Ferrini's books are the most important I have read.
I study them like a Bible.

ELISABETH KÜBLER-ROSS

Paul Ferrini's writing will inspire you to greater insights
and understandings, to more clarity and a grander resolve
to make changes in your life that can truly change the world.

NEALE DONALD WALSCH

Paul Ferrini is an important teacher in the new millenium.
Reading his work has been a major awakening for me.

IYANLA VANZANT

Paul Ferrini is a modern day Kahlil Gibran — poet, mystic,
visionary, teller of truth.

LARRY DOSSEY

I feel that this work comes from a continuous friendship with the
deepest part of the Self. I trust its wisdom.

COLEMAN BARKS

Paul Ferrini reconnects us to the Spirit Within,
to that place where even our deepest wounds can be healed.

JOAN BORYSENKO

Paul Ferrini's wonderful books show us a way to walk lightly
with joy on planet Earth.

GERALD JAMPOLSKY

Please visit our website for more information:
www.paulferrini.com
www.lightforthesoul.com

ISBN # 978-1-879159-99-0

Manufactured in the United States of America

Crossing the Threshold

from *FEAR*

to *LOVE*

31 DAYS OF SPIRITUAL AWAKENING

Paul Ferrini

TABLE OF CONTENTS

_____

Opening the Doors
to Love's Presence

There are many doors to unconditional love. Entering any one of these doors makes it easier for us to enter the others. Cultivating one core spiritual virtue helps us to cultivate all the others.

When you have experienced love's patient blessing on an imperfect world, you know have come home, and you welcome all who would enter, no matter which door they use to enter.

In this world, we are all brothers and sisters. We may have a different color skin, speak a different language, or practice a different religion, but these differences cannot undermine our equality unless we allow them to.

You and I are the door keepers. Turn anyone away and you may find that the door closes to you too. How we treat others determines the quality of the life we live here. The core spiritual virtues discussed in this book bring us closer

_____

to God and to each other. Cultivating these virtues is the work of a lifetime. It requires constant practice and, fortunately, life provides us with many challenges and opportunities to practice.

We may not know how to love without conditions when we come into this world, but we can use our time here to learn to open our hearts to love's presence. We can learn to speak the language of love and to embody love in our actions toward others.

To be sure, we will make mistakes and we will have to learn to forgive ourselves and others. As long as forgiveness is our compass and constant companion, we cannot lose our way back home.

31 DAYS OF SPIRITUAL PRACTICE

Why are there 31 Teachings and Practices in this book? Because each month has a maximum of 31 days and so there is a Teaching and a Practice for every day of the month.

Think of your first month of practice as a 31-day spiritual retreat. Of course, you don't have to travel to a monastery or retreat center. You don't need to leave your home or your job. You just need to create time and space within your life to focus on the Teaching and Practice for that day.

Read the Teaching and the Practice when you get up in the morning. Consider how the Teaching applies to your life now and in the past. Pay attention to the Opposite States of Consciousness listed. You may experience one or more these during the day, and they will point you clearly toward the correction that needs to be made.

Ponder the teaching throughout the day, using every opportunity to engage in the practice for that day. If you have time, write your reflections in your journal at the end of the day.

Each day of practice will bring its own unique insight. Yet there is a cumulative effect. Every day of practice creates momentum and results in a deeper and more profound experience. If you can stay with this process for 31 days, you may be pleasantly surprised at the results.

If you miss a day, don't worry or beat yourself up. Just pick up the thread on the next day.

NON-CALENDAR VS. CALENDAR-BASED APPROACH

In some ways the non-calendar based approach is the easiest way to begin this practice because you can start right away with #1 and continue daily until you come to day #31. Then, if you want to continue, you can either repeat the process or switch to the calendar-based approach. I suggest this method for beginners.

When using a calendar-based approach, you read the text associated with the specific day of the month. If you begin on February 27, then you read text #27. If you begin on April 3, you read text #3. Some months have only 30 days, so there will be no text for day #31 in those months. In February, there will be no text for day #29 (unless it is a leap year) or day #30.

A calendar-based approach works best when you use this process over several consecutive months. It also enables you to check in on any given day in the future, even if you are not practicing every day.

One way to combine the two methods is simply to start on the first day of the month.

ONGOING PRACTICE

If you find this practice helpful, let it become an ongoing one. Every month you have the opportunity to revisit each of the Teachings/Practices and integrate it more deeply into your life.

Each day look for the opportunities life brings to you to cross the threshold. When the door opens, however, unexpectedly, walk through it.

In this way, you create a simple daily practice that can transform your consciousness and your life. You invite the Spirit of God to enter into your heart and mind, to speak with your lips and reach out with your hands.

As your heart opens, your cup is filled to overflowing and you become a fountainhead, offering acceptance and love to all who encounter you.

Namaste,

Paul Ferrini

When you have experienced love's patient blessing on an imperfect world, you know you have come home, and you welcome all who would enter, no matter which door they use.

DAY 1

———

Acceptance

Acceptance is a state of consciousness. We cultivate acceptance when we accept life as it is and people as they are. We don't have to like something to accept it. The more we accept life as it unfolds with all its polarities—light and dark, good and bad, up and down, persona and shadow—the more we begin to create integration and cohesion within the psyche.

OPPOSITE STATES OF CONSCIOUSNESS: Rejection, Denial, Resistance, Projection. When you reject something, react in fear, or project your thoughts and feelings onto others, you create division in the psyche and conflict in the world.

Acceptance is the door to love without conditions. Without the practice of acceptance, only conditional love is possible. You accept only what supports your ego structure and reject or resist everything else. What you reject or resist comes back to haunt you. It challenges you to open your heart and your mind.

Life is forever asking you for acceptance. You might not like something. You may be threatened by it. You may be triggered. But there it is staring you in the face. Try to push it away or bury it and it comes back stronger.

What you accept becomes integrated. The part is absorbed into the whole. But what you do not accept is like a wedge that would divide the whole into thousands of pieces. Acceptance leads to integration. Lack of acceptance leads to separation and division.

It is a common misconception that you must like something to accept it. Liking something means that your ego structure is not threatened by it. When you like something it is easy to accept it. But acceptance does not become a spiritual virtue until someone or something you don't like shows up. That is when your ego is challenged. That is when your spiritual work begins.

When faced with what you do not like, simply allow it to be. Do not fight it. Do not resist it. Do not try to make it go away. Do not run away and hide from it. Simply see it and acknowledge it. Say "this is something that triggers me" or "this is something I have trouble accepting." Only when you acknowledge lack of acceptance does accepting something you do not like become possible. But acknowledging is just the beginning of a process that leads to acceptance.

Once you acknowledge the difficulty, you ask, "How can I be with this? How can I be present with the feelings that are coming up without resisting, defending or running away? How can I get my arms around it? How can I see it in a different way, not as an attack or a punishment, but as an opportunity to grow and deepen my capacity to love?"

The irony is that acknowledging your lack of acceptance is the path toward acceptance. When you see that you do not accept, that there is something you react negatively to, you are forced to look at your shadow. You are asked to see your shame or fear directly.

We think that shame and fear are bad, but they are not bad. They are just unintegrated aspects of consciousness and experience, parts of ourselves we have not yet learned to love. They are coming up now, because it is time for us to open our hearts and minds and embrace all of who we are.

We need to understand that others are mirrors for us. When we push them away because we feel triggered or threatened, we are also pushing away unintegrated aspects of ourselves that they mirror to us.

We need to embrace the little child within who feels angry or sad. We cannot continue to abandon him, even though he is not very "likeable." He is filled with fear and shame. He hides from us or lashes out. We feel disconnected from him already. Pushing him away, not answering his call for love, just makes matters worse.

Everyone who triggers us gives us the opportunity to

bring love to the child within. By accepting others as they are, even when they behave badly, we are telling the child that we can accept him too, even when he is reacting in fear, raging out or withdrawing into his dark cave.

Bringing acceptance to what happens creates safety for the child within. It lets him know that he is not alone and that nothing that he has said or done can cut him off from our love.

It is through our acceptance and love that the child is reborn out of pain. Ours is a journey of emotional healing. Everyone of us travels this path. There is no one here who has not been wounded or does not need to heal.

All have been betrayed, ostracized, abandoned. And all must be led out of fear and shame back to our original innocence.

THE PRACTICE

Today, see what you cannot accept, what you resist, judge, fear and turn away from. You think of this as "other," or outside of you, but it is really a reflection of something inside that you are unable to embrace.

When you accept and bring love to your shadow self, integration happens in the psyche. Divergent and discordant aspects of self come back together. You become more whole.

So today bring love and acceptance to the child within. Do not reject or abandon him/her. Realize that others who trigger you are mirroring back to you parts of yourself that have split off and need to be integrated. When you bring acceptance and love, integration and healing happen. So today, let this be your prayer: "Allow me to see the parts of myself that I have not yet learned to love. Allow me to open my heart to my own fear and shame so that I can walk through the door you would open to me. Allow me to know and understand that no part of me is bad or unredeemable. Allow me to see and accept my brothers and sisters as they are, for they are experiencing the same psychological division and emotional pain that I am."

Today learn to see what you have difficulty accepting without looking through the lens of fear and shame. Have the courage to be present with the circumstances that challenge you. Being aware of what you do not accept is the doorway to acceptance. So don't beat yourself up with this awareness. Use it to bring love to the child within who feels abandoned or rejected.

Notice when others do not accept you or are triggered by something that you say or do. Do not react to their rejection of you by rejecting them. That will not make it easier for you to accept yourself or to accept them. Accept that they do not accept you. Accept that they are triggered, that they have fear or shame coming up and be gentle with them as you would be gentle with your own child.

JOURNALING QUESTIONS

What is the most difficult thing for me to accept?

Have I learned to accept some person or situation that I do not like or that has triggered me in the past?

DAY 2

———

Forgiveness

Forgiveness is a state of consciousness. We cultivate forgiveness when we forgive ourselves and others. We all know that we are supposed to forgive, and we may even be willing, but we cannot forgive until we are ready. Forgiveness is a process that takes time and often happens over months and years, not over days or weeks. Learning to forgive requires that we see and dissolve the blocks to forgiveness in our hearts and minds. There is always a payback for not forgiving others or ourselves. We need to see what they payback is and to realize that it is holding us back from healing and taking back our power.

OPPOSITE STATES OF CONSCIOUSNESS: Blaming, Shaming, Retaliating, or Holding a grudge/grievance against others. Not forgiving others means living as a victim and giving our power away. It prevents us from healing. Feeling guilt for our words/actions and blaming/shaming ourselves is also a major block to our healing. Punishing ourselves does not help us learn from our mistakes and bring correction. It just keeps our wounds alive.

THE TEACHING

Forgiveness is one of the most important teachings and practices on our spiritual path. Without forgiveness things that are broken stay broken. Trust is destroyed. Revenge, retaliation and guilt carry the day.

Without forgiveness there can be no correction or redemption. Wounds fester and healing is not possible.

Human beings can live without forgiveness only in a mistake free world, in world without attack or punishment, in a world where one brother or sister cannot or does not trespass against another.

Such a world exists only in Heaven or Paradise, in the Garden before the Fall. As soon as a single mistake or trespass occurs in Paradise the fall from grace is automatic. It just happens, usually unconsciously.

On the other hand, when there is a fall, there is also an atonement, a rebirth, a resurrection. But that is not automatic. It is a conscious process that requires learning from our mistakes, correcting them, and forgiving our trespasses.

In the Lord's prayer given to us by Jesus, we ask God to forgive our trespasses and we affirm our willingness to forgive the trespasses of others. By forgiving ourselves and others, our lifeline to the divine is restored. Redemption is possible for ourselves and others. Guilt is dissolved and grace restored.

Jesus gave us the Lord's prayer for a reason. He knew that we, like our ancestors Adam and Eve, were going to make mistakes. Fear would rise up and we would strike out against our brother. Cain would slay Able. Wounds and the fear and shame attached to them would proliferate. We would attack each other, sometimes mercilessly.

To forgive each other, we do not have to forget what happened. As Elie Wiesel and others have pointed out, remembering what happened helps us avoid repeating it. But remembering does not have to mean keeping the wound alive or seeking to avenge it, because that bitterness destroys all the joy in our lives. We must forgive, not just to release others from hell, but also to release ourselves.

Bishop Tutu understood the importance of both remembering and forgiving in helping to create the Truth Commission in South Africa. Those who had been brutalized and oppressed were given the opportunity to confront their oppressors, to bear witness to their pain, to speak their truth and have their voices be heard. The guilt of the victimizers was exposed without equivocation or apology. But the guilty were not executed or beaten. They were forced to come to terms with the pain and suffering they had caused so that they could ask for and receive forgiveness, so that seeds of racism could be plucked out of their hearts and minds, one person at a time.

Turning the other cheek does not mean that you forget. It does not mean that you back down and remain a victim. On the contrary. It requires that you find your voice, that you learn to stand up for yourself and be seen and heard. All this is necessary. As I have said many times, there is no forgiveness without correction.

Correction prepares the ground so that the seeds of forgiveness can be sown. When our errors are seen, when we learn from our mistakes, then forgiveness can take root. Otherwise, forgiveness is shallow or insincere.

Being sorry is not enough. It is only a first step. It must lead to a change in consciousness and behavior. You must find the root of racism and hatred within your heart and mind. False beliefs must be exposed and uprooted. Lies must be confronted and truth must proclaimed, from the gutter and from the rooftop.

Change will not happen in the world until it happens within our hearts and minds. Until peace comes to your heart and mine, swords will not be turned into plowshares.

THE TRUTH ABOUT FORGIVENESS

The truth is that you cannot make yourself forgive. Forgiveness cannot happen by force. You can forgive only when you are willing and when you are ready.

So we all must be honest with ourselves. Sometimes we are simply not willing to forgive and any attempt to forgive will be a sham. It will be a wolf in sheep's clothing. So let us refrain from that charade. Let us be with the awareness that we are not willing and investigate why that is. What fear or shame in us is feeding our desire for revenge or our nursing of a grievance?

If we are willing to look at our own shadow material, we may see how there is a pay-off for remaining a victim. If

I am convinced that you are the cause of my pain or unhappiness, then I can hold you hostage and I don't have to take responsibility for my own healing. It may take a while of spinning my wheels and going around the rosy before I realize that I cannot heal or regain my joy until I am willing to take you off the hook.

And even once I am willing, forgiveness may not happen quickly or easily. It may take time and continued awareness. When I realize that I am not ready to climb the mountain of forgiveness, I have to start by taking baby steps. Then I can step forward and make my peace with the journey. Forgiveness happens at its own pace, as I am ready, as false beliefs fall away and my heart opens. I cannot rush the process.

When I become impatient with the process, I fall back. I lose the trail and it takes even longer to find it again.

Forgiveness may be my goal, and it is a worthy goal, but it is a process as well. And the process is as important as the goal. Indeed, without the process, the goal cannot be reached.

I may want to forgive. I may be willing. But there may be blocks to forgiveness that I have to see and overcome before genuine forgiveness can happen.

In that sense, we are all on the path to forgiveness. We are not there yet. There is always another step beyond the one we have taken. We need to be at peace with the process to reach the goal.

FORGIVING OTHERS AND FORGIVING OURSELVES

Forgiving others and forgiving ourselves are two sides of the same coin. If I am unable to forgive you, then it is not possible for me to forgive myself. The more I blame you, the more I condemn myself and bring shame on my inner child. So I must understand that forgiving you is the doorway to forgiving myself.

On the other hand, it may be easier for me to forgive you than it is for me to forgive myself. I may continue to feel shame and guilt for my words and actions even when you have forgiven me. Holding onto my shame and punishing myself may be easier for me than learning my lessons and changing my behavior. I must ask, "If I have not forgiven myself, have I really forgiven you, or have I just suppressed my anger at you so I don't have to confront you?"

If I am not honest with you about my anger, if I don't stand up for myself or my feelings, then my fear and timidity encourage you to encroach again. This can be a vicious cycle.

In order for me to heal and step into my power forgiveness must flow both ways. Forgiveness is not genuine or deep unless and until I take both of us off the hook.

THE PRACTICE

Today be honest with yourself. See where you are willing to forgive yourself and others and where you are not. Don't hide behind the ideal of forgiveness and then beat yourself up because you cannot reach it. Don't try to eat the whole steak. Bite off a piece you can chew.

Today understand the forgiveness is a process that usually takes weeks, months, even years. You cannot force yourself to forgive or rush the process. You have to take one step at a time.

Tell the truth to yourself and acknowledge when you are not ready to forgive. Seeing where you can't forgive gives you a roadmap. It shows you the next step on the journey. Be patient and take that step when you are ready.

Today stand up for yourself and tell your truth when others are trespassing against you. Telling them is important and does not have to involve blame or retaliation. If you are afraid to stand up for yourself, be aware that you are complicit in the trespass because you allow yourself to be victimized. That becomes your lesson.

When you stand up, you stop being a victim. You help others take responsibility for their aggressive actions and you make it less likely that they will attack you again.

Today, be aware when you are feeling guilty and beating yourself up for something you said or did. Don't wallow in guilt. It isn't helpful to you or anyone else. Confess your guilt and move on. Atone. Learn your lessons. Make amends or restitution. Holding onto your guilt prevents healing from happening for you and encourages others to keep you on the hook. That retards their healing as well. It is a no-win situation.

Today, apologize, learn from your mistake and then take yourself off the hook. Practice self-forgiveness, knowing that forgiving yourself and forgiving others are two sides of the same coin.

JOURNALING QUESTIONS

What is the most difficult thing for me to forgive myself for?
What am I having difficulty forgiving others for?

DAY 3

———

Humility

Humility is a state of consciousness. We cultivate humility when we emphasize our equality with others, refuse to puff ourselves up, inflate our abilities or accomplishments, and allow others to share in the credit we receive for our creative endeavors. Because we step back and appreciate what others bring to the table, people feel connected to us and happy to cooperate with us. By letting others go first, we are treated with deference and respect. Because we do not call attention to ourselves, ask for favors or special treatment, others sing our praises and invite us to come forward and lead.

OPPOSITE STATES OF CONSCIOUSNESS: Hubris, Narcissism, Arrogance, Self-importance, Excessive pride, Asking for special treatment, Puffing ourselves up at the expense of others, Needing to be the star of the show and the center of attention.

THE TEACHING

Jesus told us the first shall be last and the last shall be first. The teaching is very clear. A humble person does not puff himself up, compare himself to others at their expense, or parade his wisdom or accomplishments. Instead of seeking credit, he gives credit to others. As a result, others feel appreciated and welcome him. While he appears to dim his light so that others may shine, those who are wise see that wherever he goes, there is more light in the room.

This is one of the paradoxes of the spiritual path. The more we need recognition/credit from others, the hungrier we are for praise, the less we receive. People are repelled by us. They can feel that we are like a big emotional vacuum that wants to suck up their energy.

On the other hand, when we know our self-worth internally, we do not have to seek for validation from others. By making ourselves small and insignificant, most people overlook us. That way we keep ourselves free of their ego agendas with all their unnecessary entanglements. Only those who are earnest and wise notice us. They become our students and helpers. As a result, many wonderful things are accomplished, even though it seems that we do little or nothing.

Most of have a deep-seated feeling that we are not enough and that we need to *be more* or *get more* to gain the acceptance of others. So we try very hard to distinguish ourselves from others, to prove our worth, to make others like us or need us. But this strategy inevitably fails. Feeling lack inside, we actually push away the attention we seek. Nothing can fill the hole in our hearts. The only people who respond to our desperate need for love are the people who like us have no love to give. So instead of filling up the emptiness within we actually increase the size and depth of the hole. And that makes us even more desperate to get love. It is a vicious cycle.

In the end we realize the simple spiritual law that to get love we have to give it. And we cannot give love to others if we have no love for ourselves, so we have to start at the bottom of the hole and work our way out. We have to start by learning to bring love to the little child within who does not feel lovable. That means we have to connect with the Source of Love inside ourselves. We need to find the Source so that we can become the Bringer of Love.

Until we can bring love to ourselves we will have no love to give to others and so no love will come back to us. So we must stop the useless search for the holy grail out there in the world. The grail does not exist out there. The grail abides in our heart of hearts, in our Core Self, in the place where we open to receive Love.

It is ironic, but narcissism is the opposite of love for self. The narcissist wears the mask of self-love because he pretends to be greater and more wonderful than others. But it is just a mask. Beneath the mask is emptiness and self-loathing.

He puffs himself up so that he will be noticed. But as soon as someone challenges him he reacts with fear and vengeance. He does not want anyone to try to burst his bubble, because he knows that, if and when that happens, it won't be pretty.

THE PRACTICE

Today be aware when you are puffing yourself up, making yourself more important than others, or seeking to be the center of attention. Instead of trying to be first, let others go before you. Sit at the back of the bus or give your seat to someone who needs it more than you do. Be generous, be kind, be humble. You are not the center of the universe and your needs are no more important than anyone else's.

Today stop pretending to know everything. Realize that what you don't know is much greater than what you do know. Be okay with not knowing. When people ask for directions and you don't know the way, say "Sorry I can't guide you there. I have never been there."

Don't inflate yourself or inflate the expectations that others have of you. Promise only what you know that you can deliver. Or better still promise less, so that people will be delighted when you give them more than you promised. By making yourself last you actually move ahead in the line. By hiding your light, it increases by itself. You don't have to make it happen. It just happens by itself.

This is not an easy teaching to practice. Those who have big egos simply cannot do it. They go to the Guru expecting special treatment, and he tells them to go to the basement and clean the toilets. Instead of learning humility, they feel shamed and humiliated. They feel inferior and that makes them act superior to others. People eventually catch on to that charade and stop catering to them. In the end, they either surrender to the teaching, or they leave and continue their ego-inflated search elsewhere.

Without humility progress cannot be made on the spiritual path. Grandiosity and spiritual pride are major obstacles to the process of awakening. They simply feed the ego. And when the ego is running our spiritual path, shame and humiliation is bound to follow. Those who puff themselves up will have their bubble burst. Those who put themselves up on a pedestal will be pulled down into the street. Better to learn the lessons of humility now and avoid the drama.

JOURNALING QUESTIONS

In what ways do you need to be more humble in your life?

Do you or anyone you know have Narcissistic tendencies that need to be addressed by establishing healthy boundaries?

DAY 4

———

Patience

Patience is a state of consciousness. We cultivate patience when we refuse to put pressure on ourselves or others and allow life to unfold organically in its own time and place. We put our ego agenda aside and pay attention to the signs and clues that suggest the best direction for our energies. The more patient we are the more progress we make on our spiritual path, because we stop swimming against the tide, exhausting our energy. Instead we wait to catch the wave so that the momentum is on our side and we can move forward without contention or struggle.

OPPOSITE STATES OF CONSCIOUSNESS: Impatience, Anxiety, Rushing, Forcing, Putting pressure on ourselves or others. When this occurs, it is time to slow down, drop our ego agenda, come into our hearts, and become present emotionally with life as it is. As *A Course in Miracles* says, "Only infinite patience brings immediate results."

THE TEACHING

We all have our ego agendas. We want to make things happen, get things accomplished, solve our problems and achieve our goals. But sometimes the outcome we are emotionally invested in simply isn't going to happen. That may be because the outcome is not in harmony with who we are, or it may be because the timing is not right. Either way, our progress is blocked.

Sometimes we are too inflexible and unwilling to negotiate and that creates a log jam in the flow of creative energy. In order for us to manifest what is positive for ourselves and others, we have to be clear on our goals, but flexible in the way we reach them. We have to be emotionally present, willing and able to move forward and so must others. When we are not ready or others are not ready, the way forward will be blocked or obscured.

If we are clear about our goal and committed to it, we can get in touch with the blocks in our consciousness and work to remove them. When we get out of the way and surrender our agendas and expectations, the flow can often be restored. Of course, this takes time, vigilance and patience with the process.

If we try to rush the process, it will abort or shut down. We simply cannot make things happen. What happens by force is wound-driven and results in negative consequences for us and others.

So there are times when we have to get off our hurry horse and take baby steps. We need to slow things down and tune into how we feel. Are we pushing forward with blinders on? Are we stuck in our heads and disconnected from our hearts?

Sometimes the obstacles appear to be outside of us, but when we look deeply we realize that the outside block is just a reflection of an inside one. So we have to take our attention away from the world and reconnect to our hearts before attempting to move forward. Then, the universe will let us know if we are back on track, because our progress will continue. The way will open before us.

Being patient means taking the time to check within, asking "Does this feel right?" And if the answer is "No" revising our expectations or our course of action.

Things get done when it is time for them to get done, not necessarily when we want them to get done. We are not in control of what or when something happens. To be sure, we have input, but so do other people and so does the energy that has already been set in motion based on past thoughts and actions.

In the end, there is a right time and a wrong time for everything. As we are told in Ecclesiastes, "There is a time for every season . . . a time to sow and a time to reap, a time to cast away stones and a time to gather stones together."

When it is the wrong time, we have to be patient and wait until the time is right. In spite of the belief of our impatient egos, we cannot get blood out of a stone. Banging our head or someone else's against the door does not make it open. Sometimes we have to give up, admit defeat, and surrender before the energy can change.

Patience helps us get back on track with the universal flow of energy so that we can swim with the tide, instead of against it. When we stop forcing and get of the way, the energy picks up again and we can dance with life.

This dance continues every day. We move out of the flow and back into it. And the more patient we are, the better we sense when it is time to move and when it is time to wait. Little by little, we learn to catch the tide and ride the waves. Being in flow is so much more satisfying than being out of the flow and stuck in the mud or jammed against a rock.

After a few times of being beaten up in the river, we stop fighting it and learn to cooperate. That saves us and others a lot of grief. When we stay present and let go, we reach our goals without a huge effort.

THE PRACTICE

Today be aware when you become anxious and lose your patience. You can't practice being patient until you are aware that you have lost your patience. Be aware of the signs. Are you nervous. worried, beginning to panic? Are you rushing around? Are thoughts spinning around in your head? Are you preoccupied with negative experiences in the past or afraid of repeating them in the future?

If so, take a deep breath in and let it go. Do this several times, allowing yourself to calm down, get out of your head and into your heart. Let your energy flow all the way down from the top of your head into the bottoms of your feet. Wiggle your toes and feel the energy of the ground beneath you. This helps you to get grounded and become emotionally present with your experience here and now.

Now take a moment to tune into what fear is rising up and causing your anxiety. Hold that fear in compassionate awareness. You do not have to try to make it go away. Just hold it gently as you breathe with it.

Become aware of how you are putting pressure on yourself or others. Notice when you are trying to avoid or rush through some situation that makes you uncomfortable. Ask yourself: "How can I accept what is happening now and relax into it? What are some ways that I can be more patient with myself or with others?"

Then go back to what you were doing with more peace and acceptance in your heart. Do what you can do. Say what you can say. And what you cannot say or do leave for another day. Don't try to make something happen that is not ready to happen. Don't pick the fruit before it is ripe. Wait for the right time.

Swim with the current of the river, not against it. Then you will not exhaust yourself or make foolish mistakes. And remember, when a storm comes up, it is better to wait it out on the riverbank then to dive into the rapids. Speeding up causes unnecessary hazards and potential harm to yourself and others.

JOURNALING QUESTIONS

Where (and with whom) do I need to learn to be more patient?

How can I take the pressure off myself and others and allow life to unfold?

DAY 5

———

Gentleness

Gentleness is a state of consciousness. We cultivate gentleness when we refuse to beat ourselves up or to be harsh with others. When we are gentle we accept our humanness. We know that no one is perfect and we all make mistakes. So when errors are made, we try to learn from them and we do not blame and shame ourselves or others. The more gentle we are, the more understanding and forgiveness we experience in our lives, and the easier it is to acknowledge and correct our mistakes.

OPPOSITE STATES OF CONSCIOUSNESS: Perfectionism, pressure, harshness, criticism. Intolerance, punishment, lack of forgiveness. When we see that we are being hard on ourselves and others, we need to recognize our human imperfection and bring compassion instead of shame and blame. We need soften, open our hearts, and be gentle with ourselves and others.

THE TEACHING

When fear arises, we all lash out against others. We are harsh or unkind. We may even be brutal. Our behavior toward others stems from a deep shame and unworthiness. Not only do we judge, attack and punish others; we also judge, condemn and are often merciless toward ourselves.

We mistakenly believe that we have to perfect to get the love and attention we want. Perfection, of course, is an impossible goal, and the more we expect ourselves or others to be perfect, the more blame and shame we carry and project onto others. The result is a very harsh and unforgiving world.

Each one of us has to learn to accept our human imperfection and that of others. We have to realize that mistakes are part of the learning process. They don't condemn us. Instead they offer us opportunities to grow and take responsibly for our thoughts, feelings, words and actions.

Being gentle with ourselves and others is one of the key steps toward forgiveness. When we soften and stop shaming and blaming, when we see our trespasses and errors with empathy and compassion for each other, our relationships become kinder and more supportive. We learn how to get along as equals, with caring and mutual respect. We stop being warlords and become peacemakers.

Being kind and gentle seems to be a no-brainer. All our religions tell us to be kind and gentle, to treat others as we would like them to treat us. But often we do this only in a superficial way. We are polite to people's faces and then gossip behind their backs. We are gentle with the ones we like, the people who share our language, our culture, our religion. But we are very harsh with those who are different from us, and even harsher with those who challenge our beliefs.

We must learn to go deeper. We must learn to accept and respect those who are different from us, those who have another experience or a different set of beliefs. It isn't easy to see how we are triggered by these people, and how we speak and act toward them in ways that are harsh and intolerant. But we must see where we are biased, strident and unfair. We must see our own blocks to love and acceptance as they reveal themselves.

We need to face our shadow material when it rises up. Otherwise, we will continue to project our shame and fear onto others. Violence, distrust, and segregation will be the norm.

By learning to see our wounded child with compassion, we bring love to the parts of ourselves that feel unlovable. That means that we soften inside. Our rough edges begin to dissolve. As we feel more lovable and acceptable as an imperfect human being, we extend the same compassion to others.

Begin gentle with ourselves extends outward to others. And being gentle with others helps us to internalize that quality, so that we stop criticizing our inner child, and bring acceptance and love instead.

Most of us can be very hard on ourselves. So we must learn to ease up and take the pressure off. We need to stop trying to be perfect or to be better than others. It is okay to be who we are and sometimes that means we come in second or third in the race. We might even come in last. If we can love ourselves even when we struggle or fail, we can win the ultimate battle of life: learning to love and accept ourselves unconditionally.

Being hard on ourselves may deflect our judgments away from others and turn our anger inward toward ourselves. This may take others off the hook, but often it leads to co-dependence. It keeps the narcissism alive in others and reinforces our own victimhood. Our self-deprecation and our lack of self-esteem feed the Narcissist's grandiosity. In contrast to us, he is always the best and the brightest and we continue to invite him to shine at our expense.

When we are timid or intimidated by the power of others, and afraid to stand up for ourselves, we stay locked in our fear and shame. We continue to beat ourselves up and to feel powerless to free ourselves from our emotional prison.

In this case, our primary lesson is to learn to be gentle with ourselves and to put ourselves in environments in which we are encouraged to speak up and be seen and heard. It may seem ironic, but in our case standing up to others can be a powerful way to be kind, gentle and nurturing to ourselves.

THE PRACTICE

Today try to get in touch with what is most challenging for you. Is your biggest challenge to learn to be gentle and encouraging toward others? Or is your biggest challenge to be gentle with yourself?

If you have difficulty being gentle with others learn to stand back and take up less space in the room. Allow others to breathe the air and be seen and heard. If you are gentle with others but merciless toward yourself, have the courage to reveal yourself and refuse to be overshadowed by those who like to be the center of attention.

As the events of the day unfold, notice when fear or shame arises and you either jump in with both feet or shrink back and hide. If your pattern is to shrink back and hide, practice gentleness by taking baby steps forward. You cannot emerge from victim consciousness unless you risk being seen and heard.

Be patient and give yourself credit for each baby step you take. Don't put pressure on yourself, but don't be intimidated either.

As you can see, there is a kind of balance that is needed here between the extremes of being gentle and being strong. Those who are overly strong must learn to gentle with others. And those who are overly meek must learn to stand up to others and be gentle with themselves.

As the meek become stronger and the strong become more gentle, balance is achieved. Then, masculine and feminine qualities can abide in all of us. Men can be gentle. Women can be strong. Integration happens and we can experience greater success in our relationships.

JOURNALING QUESTIONS

In what ways am I beating myself up?

How am I being harsh with others?

How can I learn to stand up for myself and be less harsh with others?

DAY 6

———

Honesty

Honesty is a state of consciousness. We cultivate honesty when we tell the truth even when it is difficult. Of course, to tell the truth to others, we must first know it for ourselves, so honesty begins in our own consciousness and then extends to others. By being honest with others, we encourage them to be honest with us.

OPPOSITE STATES OF CONSCIOUSNESS: Lying, Deception, Fabricating, Hiding, Denying or Obscuring the truth. When we recognize that we are not telling the truth, we need to acknowledge it to ourselves and then to others. If we are not sure what is true, we have to be willing to admit that.

We have been told many times that "honesty is the best policy," yet it is often difficult for us to be honest with others. Rather than tell an uncomfortable truth, we tell others what we think they want to hear. This may avoid conflict temporarily but it just kicks the can down the road. Sooner or later the truth will come out.

If your partner asks you, "Do you still love me?" and you say "Yes" when the truth is "No," you are being dishonest. Maybe you are afraid your partner will leave or have an affair if he or she knows the truth, so you lie to protect yourself. But then perhaps you are the one who has an affair and then you get caught and the truth comes out. Is this the way you want to end your relationship? Wouldn't is be better to say, "My feelings for you are not the same as they were before" and let that be the entrée to a longer, more heartfelt conversation?

Or maybe the honest answer is "I don't know. I am feeling a bit confused or ambivalent."

When you tell others the truth you are showing them respect. You are refusing to play games with them or to keep them guessing. While the truth can be difficult to hear, it is also empowering because it lets other people know where they stand.

When the truth is spoken no one is kept in the dark. No one has a secret or an unfair advantage. When both people tell each other the truth, all the cards are put on the table.

Telling the truth is the first and most important step. It does not mean that you know what to do with all those cards. It doesn't mean you are ready to make a major decision. It just puts everything out into the open so that things can be discussed and eventually a decision can be made.

Sometimes the truth that you speak is not the whole truth, because you don't know how you really feel. You may say "No I don't love you," when the truth is that you want more intimacy with your partner and you don't know how to ask for it.

Maybe the truth leads to a decision to separate for a while and during that time you find you that you really do love your partner but you needed time to yourself to heal or get clear.

Telling the truth opens the door to more honest communication and more authentic behavior. That is the upside.

The downside is that it overturns the applecart. It insures that the veil of denial or secrecy is lifted and dysfunctional patterns of self-betrayal and co-dependence are revealed.

It is one of our human weaknesses to want to hold onto the past even when we know that it is not working. And the way we hold on is by denying or hiding the truth, first from ourselves and then from others. That is our way of keeping the past in place, even when our soul is screaming for change.

In the end, our soul wins out over any attempt we make to deny our true needs and feelings. We cannot build a life on lies and deception. If we try, the house of cards we build will come tumbling down. Lies and deception lead to larger and more destructive consequences. Better to have the courage to face the truth now, when change can happen with reasonable safety, then to wait until the stakes become too high.

It is not uncommon to read in the news how someone goes completely off his rocker and murders his wife and children. Why did he wait until the dynamite was lit to acknowledge the truth to himself and others? That, I am afraid, is the inevitable consequence of living in denial.

In our Affinity Process we ask people to tell the truth to each other without blaming or shaming each other. We ask people to speak and listen from the heart so that they can learn what is real for the other person.

This process makes it possible to get everything out on the table. Its intent is not to negotiate or try to make decisions. That can happen later.

So when I use the Affinity Process, I might say "I am feeling confused and ambivalent about our marriage. I am feeling depressed and cut off from you and from myself." That tells you something really important about what is going on for me.

I don't blame you for what I am feeling. I don't try to make it your fault or your responsibility. I simply acknowledge what is going on for me, even though it is not pleasant to say.

And now you know what is going on for me and you don't have to try to fix it or make it better; you can just let it in and be with it. And, if you are ready, you can tell me honestly what is going on for you. You could say, for example, "I have been noticing how distant you have been and I have been feeling that it is my fault and I must be doing something wrong. I have even wondered if you still love me. I have been afraid to speak about it for fear that you would withdraw even more."

And I can acknowledge that without trying to reassure you or fix anything for you. We can both feel grateful that the truth has been spoken and no one has been blamed or shamed. Now I am aware of what is going on for you and you are aware of what is going on for me and we can let it all settle in.

When we are ready we can tell each other more. We can even explore what our options are. But that can happen only when we have given the truth time to work in your consciousness and mine.

The beauty is that the walls of denial have been taken down. No one is avoiding the truth or hiding it. We are naked now, face to face. In that there is equality and mutual respect.

Now, when it is time to build, we will not be building a life of lies. We will not be building on quick sand. We will be building on bedrock, on the truth of who we are. We will be building on solid ground.

THE PRACTICE

Today be aware when you are not being honest, when you are hiding or disguising the truth. Notice when you tell people what you think they want to hear, instead of how you really feel. And when you catch yourself, stop and see if it is possible for you to be more authentic.

Today also notice when others are not being authentic with you. Ask them "Do you really mean that?" or "Is that how you really feel." Let other people know that you would rather have the truth, even if it is difficult to hear, than to be told a made-up story.

If honest communication is difficult, ask for "an affinity space," a time when you and the other person can really listen to each other without shaming and blaming. Take the time to speak and listen from the heart, to put your thoughts and feelings on the table and to listen to the experience of the other person. Remember, you are not looking for agreement here. You are just seeking understanding of what the other person is going through. And you are letting that person into your world.

No one can read a closed book, so let your book be open so that those you care about can read the truth about you. If they care, they will take the time to see and know you, and you will do the same for them.

Relationships must be nurtured and maintained. They are like a flower bed that needs water and weeding. Honesty is the water that you bring. And truth uproots the weeds so that deception cannot grow and destroy the flowers.

If you can, review your experience with this practice by writing in your journal at the end of the day. When did you deny or obscure the truth today? When did you tell people what they wanted to hear instead of telling them what you really thought and felt? When did you become aware that you were not being honest? What happened when you had the courage to speak up?

Today, was truth your friend or your enemy? Is it possible that it could be your friend even it if made you feel uneasy and uncomfortable? Did the truth shatter your mask and dissolve your story or someone else's? Did it blast open the door to your self-created prison of lies and deception or someone else's?

JOURNALING QUESTION

With whom and in what situation am I challenged to be more honest with myself and the people I love?

DAY 7

———

Generosity

Generosity is a state of consciousness. We cultivate it by being generous to others, by being willing to share our resources, instead of hoarding them or keeping them to ourselves. By giving to others, we help them to be productive and this benefits the community in which we live. In time, what we have given returns to us in full measure, whether it be through the gratitude and appreciation of others, or through the actual flow of resources back to us.

OPPOSITE STATES OF CONSCIOUSNESS: Hoarding, Stinginess, Being Cheap or Miserly, Stealing, Scamming, Cheating or misappropriating the resources of others. When we recognize that we have more than we need and are withholding resources that others need, it is time to open our hearts and give what is needed. As we give, we open ourselves to receive and energy is re-circulated.

THE TEACHING

When we are fearful it is hard to be generous. We feel threatened by others who have less than us. We are afraid that they will break into our houses and steal our prized possessions and we spend a lot of time and energy trying to protect what we own.

One of the lessons we need to learn is that resources that are not shared are squandered and without purpose. If you have a hammer and don't use it, you may keep it new and shiny, but no houses are built. What good is a tool that is never used? What good is money that is never spent, shared or invested?

No economy can survive if money or resources are hoarded and kept in the hands of a chosen few. In order for an economy to thrive, money must be spent. It must be invested in new equipment, research, training, and job creation. Having money is not enough, it must be spent in a way that improves the lives of people or there will be no healthy growth.

A healthy economy constantly renews itself, so that it is stable even though there are ups and downs. Waves come but they are ridden out. A healthy economy does not yoyo between ridiculous highs and lows. It is not a boom or bust affair.

Boom or bust economies have artificial highs and lows. The highs are higher than what is real and sustainable and the lows are lower than what can be tolerated by the majority of people.

When wealth is concentrated in the top one percent of the population the conditions for economic and political collapse are created. It is not sustainable. In order to avoid catastrophe, wealth must be redistributed, through social programs that uplift the poor, as well as through the philanthropic efforts of wealthy individuals, companies, and foundations.

On a personal level, those of us who have more than we need are challenged to share our resources with those less fortunate than us. And those who have less are encouraged to speak up and ask for what we need.

In a healthy society people of means are encouraged to open their hearts and their hands to those who are needy. Companies are asked to support social programs that help those at the bottom climb the ladder of success. When the poor and the disadvantaged have opportunities and become upwardly mobile, everyone benefits. There is less social discontent, less crime, and greater safety for all. There are more people paying taxes and leading productive lives.

It is a spiritual law that we receive as we give. The more that we give in good faith the more we can receive and then we have even more to give. This is the choice that leads to abundance in our personal lives and in our world.

Yet what comes around goes around only if you pay it forward. If you try to keep your good fortune for yourself alone you will break the spontaneous flow of energy that intensifies as receivers become givers and pay it forward for the next person or generation. Then energy does not renew itself.

The cycle of abundance is broken and there is scarcity. The rich get richer and live in greater fear of losing what they have. And the poor get poorer and become more angry and resentful because their basic needs are not being met. Economic and political polarization result. People separate into different economic and political camps. Fear and mistrust rule the day.

Change comes only when one person has the courage to reach out and share what has been given to him. He or she does not have to be rich. Even a poor person can share what s/he has with others. As I have said before, it does not matter how much you have, but whether your arms are folded over your heart or extended out to others.

Generosity comes from an open heart. It is an act of love. Think of all the people who have loved and supported you in key times in your life. Parents, teachers, friends, even strangers have extended a hand to you when you needed it and changed your life for the better. Don't you want to return the favor to someone else in need?

Generosity comes when we open our hearts to others. Then giving is natural and spontaneous. It is a privilege and a joy to share with others what sustains us and makes us happy. And sharing with others intensifies the energy and extends the arc of its expression, like ripples reaching out across the water.

THE PRACTICE

Today, imagine that you have abundant resources so that it will not be a fearful proposition to share them with others. Today use every opportunity that arises to be generous toward others. Be generous not just with your money, but with your time and your attention. When someone needs something and you have it, give it gladly. Be grateful to the universe for giving you the opportunity to help. Be aware of how helping others keeps your heart open and enables the energy to renew itself and eventually return to you.

Today, notice when fear rises up and you feel yourself contracting and withholding your resources from others. See if you can soften and come back into your heart. See if you can make eye contact with others. See if you can breathe though your fear and remain emotionally present. Ask yourself, "Is there something here that I can give? Is there something I can do or say to help?" And, if there is, say it or do it gladly.

Maybe all you can give is a smile or a few words of encouragement. Don't disparage that gift. It might be exactly what is needed. Imagine that God put you in this person's path today to cheer her up, to let her know that she is loved and appreciated. When you speak those words of encouragement, God is working through you to extend a blessing toward others.

Today see how the cycle of giving and receiving is manifesting in your life. See how the energy dwindles when you are fearful and selfish and how it comes alive when you give freely and trust there is enough here for everyone.

Today think of all the people who have paid it forward for you and see if the opportunity arises for you to do the same for someone else. If that opportunity arises, know that it is heaven-sent.

Today, you will have your own laboratory experience of scarcity and abundance. What does it feel like to shrink back or turn away from others, believing they don't deserve your help and support? What does it feel like to doubt yourself and believe that you have nothing valuable to give? On the other hand, what does it feel like to open your heart and trust that every gift you give will be helpful to someone?

Today, do not be a miser or a cheapskate. Do not hoard your resources or withhold them from others. Be generous. Give without thought of return. Pay it forward for someone else.

JOURNALING QUESTIONS

Did I have opportunities today to give my time, attention, support and assistance to others?

Did I pay it forward for someone else or give without expectation of return?

DAY 8

———

Compassion

Compassion is a state of consciousness. We cultivate compassion when we can put ourselves in someone else's situation and understand their thoughts, feelings and behavior. Our compassion helps us refrain from judgment and give others the benefit of the doubt. Even when they are expressing some strong emotion like anger, grief or jealousy, we can relate to them because we are human and have also had these feelings. Understanding and compassion go hand in hand.

OPPOSITE STATES OF CONSCIOUSNESS: Blaming, Shaming Judging, Finding fault with others. Inability to understand and accept the human frailties of other people, Callousness and Rejection, Unwillingness to offer help and encouragement. Objectifying and dehumanizing others so that we feel justified in ignoring their rights and their needs.

THE TEACHING

Compassion is similar to empathy but it is not identical. Compassion helps us to be the observer and see the big picture. It helps us understand, based on our own experience, what someone else is going through. When we feel compassion for someone, we refrain from judging or rejecting, because we can see and relate to that person's suffering.

Compassion is the bedrock of all twelve step programs. Alcoholics and drug addicts all have similar experiences. Women who have been harassed, beaten or raped have similar experiences. Boys or girls that have been abused by priests all have similar experiences. People who have been hungry or homeless understand the pain and struggle of those who are hungry and homeless now.

Our common experiences enable us to accept others even when they are acting out in unpleasant or destructive ways. We can really say, "I know, because I have been there."

Yet we can also feel compassion even if we have not had the same experience as someone else. When we understand someone's history, we can see the root cause of his transgressions, misdeeds or mistakes. A person who grows up in poverty learns to lie or steal to survive. We don't condone the lying or the stealing, but we don't write that person off and refuse to help him because we understand how he became a liar or a thief. We also can see how he might change his behavior if he were offered the resources he needs.

Compassion enables us to walk in another person's moccasins before we attempt to evaluate his behavior. Walking in his moccasins allows us to feel empathy for him. We can feel what he feels.

Empathy can be a stepping stone that deepens our experience of compassion. But it can also be problematic. When we feel empathy, we identify with that person's experience, so that it becomes our own. If that person is experiencing grief, we start to feel grief too and it triggers all the past experiences of grief we have had. Now there are two people experiencing grief, not one.

So you can see the problem. If both people are in pain, who can bring love? Who can bring healing? Who can bring encouragement?

When we identify with someone else's pain we are unable to help that person. We get stuck in the feelings. That is like one person jumping into quicksand to try to help another. It doesn't work.

So empathy is helpful only if it is short term and we use our empathy to move into compassion. Compassion sees the big picture. It helps us stand back, observe and understand the situation so that we have the ability to help.

Oftentimes, people who are empathetic have a very difficult time in life. They identify with and "take on" the feelings of others. They have to learn to establish boundaries so that they are protected from the negative feeling states of other people. They need to constantly be aware of when those boundaries are being crossed and they are jeopardizing their own comfort and safety.

Sometimes identification happens unconsciously. The people we judge harshly often bring up our own unconscious guilt. We judge the homosexual because he brings up our own gay tendencies or ambivalence about our sexuality. We think we can exorcise our own feelings by condemning those who trigger our guilt. But this never works.

In John 8.7 Jesus tells the crowd who wanted to punish the woman who had committed adultery: "He that is without sin among you, let him cast the first stone at her." Jesus calls them to a deeper level of honesty, in which they must acknowledge their own sins.

If they punish her, then they should also be punished. If they forgive her, then they can also be forgiven.

There is an essential equality that exists between all human beings. One is not better or more spiritual than another. In Christian terms, "all are sinners." All have made mistakes and must atone for them.

Compassion arises from our recognition of our essential equality with all other human beings. If I condemn others, then I am also condemning myself, for we are all cut of the same cloth.

Compassion enables me to recognize "myself in you" and "you in myself." Either both of us are guilty, or both of us are innocent. What is true for the goose is true for the gander. There is not one set of truths for you and another set of truths for me. There is just one Truth and it applies to all of us.

THE PRACTICE

Today practice compassion. Give others a break. Be tolerant toward them. Walk in their shoes and understand the struggles and pressures that they are facing in their lives. Try to find something in your own experience that helps you better understand or relate to them.

Today have compassion for yourself as well. If you are judging or condemning yourself, try to soften and cut yourself a break. You don't have to be perfect. You don't have to be right all the time. You are human and you make mistakes.

Accept your humanness and fallibility and that of all the people you interact with today. Hold your experience and that of others gently. Affirm your equality with each brother or sister you meet. See yourself in others. See others in yourself.

Even if your experience is very different from that of others, you are more like them than you are different. Find what you have in common and use that as a foundation to accept whatever differences there are.

When you see another holding a baby, think of your own child. When someone is crying, remember the last time you shed tears. When someone asks you to forgive, remember when forgiveness was offered to you.

Today remember that you are a member of one human family. It does not matter that some are tall and others short, or that some are black and others brown or white. The differences create variety and an amazing melting pot from which each emerges one-of-a-kind and unique.

One of the most beautiful paradoxes that we experience in this life is that we are both unique and the same.

We can and must individuate, but even as we discover our own truth, we do not lose our common roots. We are individuals, but also members of a family. Because of that, we are faithful to each other. We accept our differences. We support and encourage each other, even though our paths may diverge.

Today, be aware of needs of your human family. Support and encourage your brother and sister. Withhold your judgments and criticism. Give each person the respect you would want them to give to you.

Today, honor your common humanity. Understand that everyone has strengths and weaknesses. Everyone makes mistakes and is tasked to learn from them. Today, let your heart be open and extend your arms outward to bring everyone into the safety net of your love. Today, be compassionate toward all. Do not ostracize or reject anyone. Do not cast anyone out of your heart

JOURNALING QUESTIONS

In what ways do I need to be more compassionate with myself or with others?

Is empathy a stepping stone toward compassion for me or does it result in my identifying with and taking on the emotional states of others?

DAY 9

___

Detachment

Detachment is a state of consciousness. We cultivate detachment when release our attachment to someone or something that is preventing us from growing and moving forward in our lives. Detachment helps to free us from unhealthy relationships, delusional beliefs and dysfunctional behavior patterns. While emotional attachment is part of the process of learning and growing, there comes a time when we must let go to free up our energy to create something new and better in our life.

OPPOSITE STATES OF CONSCIOUSNESS: Attachment, Dependence or Co-dependence, Fixation, Identification, Merging, Submission, Obsession with people or ideas, Giving up our power to others.

Both attachment and detachment are necessary aspects of life. As a baby we are attached to our mother. We depend on her for nurturing, love and protection. But when we get older, we learn to do things for ourselves. Our father encourages us to move out into life and take greater responsibility for ourselves. Gradually, we detach from both our mother and father and claim our independence. This is a natural phenomenon.

Without detachment growth and individuation cannot take place. But detachment from parental support and authority can lead to the forming of new attachments. Perhaps we attach to a girlfriend or boyfriend, a teacher, a coach or a mentor. Our attachment enables us to receive additional support and nurturing. That is a good thing.

But there will come a time when we have to detach from that person to continue to grow. Our mentor may help us learn a skill, but once the skill is learned, we may be ready to move on to other challenges. Our apprenticeship must end for us to learn to stand on our own and become a master in our own right.

We might fall in love with someone and learn to open our heart. That is a wonderful thing, but sometimes what we can learn from each other reaches its limits, and we feel ready to move on. We realize that we will both learn more with others than we will learn by staying together. Of course, this recognition takes many forms. In other cases, there are deeper ties that bind us, but we need to take some time apart to grow before we can come back together.

Embracing and letting go are two sides of the same coin. If we get stuck in the embracing stage and do not let go, we

64   Crossing the Threshold

will not grow and individuate. On the other hand, if we get stuck in the letting go stage, we will not experience the nurturing and support that we need. After a time alone and apart, it will be time to embrace again. This is a cyclical process.

Some people have difficulty with one extreme or the other. Those who are wounded and afraid of intimacy are not good at the embracing stage. If they embrace at all it is only briefly and then they are off to the races. They may leave a trail of tears behind them. Others have difficulty with the detachment stage. They embrace easily, but then they try to hold on, even when it is clear that the time to part has come. They are often hurt and feel betrayed.

Clearly either extreme is not healthy, and fortunately most people are not extreme in their behavior. However, their lessons may lie in one stage more than the other. If you are someone who attaches and holds on, you have to learn detachment skills. If you are someone who has trouble connecting and committing, your lessons may lie in the attachment stage. You probably know which one applies to you. And you may choose a partner who exhibits the other tendency so that you can learn from him or her.

In a marriage, partners ideally help each other learn to embrace and detach as the relationship requires. Sometimes, they may need help from an outside therapist or counselor to learn the skills necessary so that the relationship can grow and thrive.

The prescription that leads to both intimacy and growth is a simple one: "Hold on tightly; let go lightly." That is what the dance of intimacy requires.

In the cycle of life, we move through various stages. In the childhood stage we are attached and dependent on others to survive. In the adult stage, we become independent and self-supporting. And then, if we decide to have children, we become caretakers and our children become dependent on us. Finally, as we move into the final stage of life, we begin to detach. We detach from work, downsize our home and simplify our lives. We prepare ourselves for the ultimate time of detachment when we will let go of the body and the world.

That is what Jesus referred to in Matthew 6:19-21, where he tells us: "Do not store up for yourselves treasures on earth, where moths and vermin destroy, and where thieves break in and steal. But store up for yourselves treasures in heaven, where moths and vermin do not destroy, and where thieves do not break in and steal. For where your treasure is, there your heart will be also."

In the end we let go of all that binds us to the world. We rest in our hearts and stay connected to love. That makes our transition out of this world easier and more graceful.

Birth and death, attachment and detachment are the alpha and omega poles of life. But even within each life, there are many smaller cycles. We breathe in and we breathe out, the sun rises and sets, the seasons come and go. We embrace each other and let go.

THE PRACTICE

Today, practice recognizing any unhealthy attachments you have. These attachments may be to people, substances (addictions) or ideas. See how these dependencies hold you back from moving forward in your life. And be prepared to start letting them go.

The first step is usually to understand what pay-offs come

from each attachment. For example, you may be attached to your job even though you don't like it because it pays the bills. You may be attached to your relationship even though there is no intimacy there, because you don't want to be lonely or you don't want to have to go to work to support yourself. You might be attached to drinking or smoking because it helps you deal with anxiety, even though you know it is taking a toll on your health. Or you might be attached to staying in a cult because it offers you "a family" to belong to, even though you have to give up your freedom to make your own choices.

If there was no pay-off, you probably would not have difficulty letting go. So you have to look carefully at the pay-off and the cost of the attachment. What is the cost of staying in a job you don't like or a marriage that offers no love or intimacy? What is the cost of an addiction that is undermining your health? What is the cost of ignoring your own guidance and giving your power away to others?

When you understand the cost is greater than the pay-off, you realize that you must take steps to free yourself from the attachment. Sometimes you can do this by standing up for yourself, speaking to your boss or your wife, going cold turkey off the booze or the tobacco, or leaving the cult. Other times it becomes clear to you that you need help from others to overcome the attachment and you take the first step by asking for the help you need.

If you are in an abusive relationship and you can't leave because you will be followed and hunted down, you might need to go to a shelter where they will place you in a safe house. If you are a heroin addict, you might need to go to a treatment center where you can be put on methadone.

Today see the cost of your attachment and take the first

step toward freedom from the entanglement. Today, pick up the phone and call for help if you need it. Today, communicate your desire for change to the people who need to hear it.

Don't remain in your victimhood because you think you have no choice. You believe that only because you have given your power away. Take your power back and take charge of your life one step at a time.

You are free to choose, but you must exercise your freedom to keep it. Don't stay in jail because you get a place to sleep and 3 meals a day. You would be better off eating dog food and sleeping under a bridge. At least you would be free to move around and find a way to a better life.

Those who give away their freedom easily slip into victim consciousness and get trapped in a prison of their own making. The longer they stay, the more docile and powerless they become. Darkness and depression set in and the light continues to recede from them.

Today check the door to your prison cell. It is not locked, even though you might have believed that it was. When you decide to leave, the door will open.

Today, detach from all that is not helpful or empowering for you and open the door to a better life. You are a creator, not a victim. The proof of that lies in the fact that you alone created the prison and you alone can escape from it.

JOURNALING QUESTION

With whom and in what situations am I challenged to detach so that I can release myself from limitations that threaten my safety, restrict my freedom, or prevent me from growing as a person?

DAY 10

———

Trust

Trust is a state of consciousness. We cultivate trust when we feel safe with a person or a situation. Then we can relax and let things unfold. Trust enables life to move forward. It is like grease on the axle of a car. All the parts move better when they are lubricated. Without trust, the parts begin to chafe and grind against each other. There is more friction, more resistance, less productivity. Trust in ourselves, trust in each other, and trust in the universe allows us to move out of struggle into grace.

OPPOSITE STATES OF CONSCIOUSNESS: Distrust, Suspicion, Resistance, Lack of confidence in self and others, Over-analysis or deliberation, Unwillingness to take a risk or let go of an unneeded restraint or protection. When we experience distrust, we need to look at the blocks to love within our own hearts. We need to understand the fear that makes us freeze up emotionally and dig our heals in, preventing change and new energy from coming in.

THE TEACHING

Trust is powerful. So is Distrust. Trust is a green light to the energy that wants to express through us. Distrust is a red light that stops the energy in its tracks so that we can take time to look around and see if anyone has our back.

Of course, if we feel unsafe, we cannot trust anyone, including ourselves. So to cultivate trust we need to create safety around us. When we know a person or a situation well, we usually feel safe, relax and trust. But if we don't know someone, we might not feel safe with that person initially. That is quite natural. Trust takes time to develop, so we must give ourselves time to be with the person or the situation until we know if we feel safe.

A very distrustful person is so injured by the past that s/he hardly ever feels safe. S/he is careful and self-protective, always waiting for the shoe to drop. Such a person does not easily experience intimacy with others and, if s/he does, it is quite limited and conditional.

Wounded and distrustful people need to go through an intensive healing process before they can begin to feel safe and trust themselves and others. Trust is always a casualty of abuse, and only as healing happens can trust in self and others be restored.

Of course, it is true that all of us are carrying childhood wounds and so we all have trust issues to some degree. For most of us, the healing process begins not by trying to trust others, but by learning to trust ourselves. That is because it is impossible to trust another person if we do not trust ourselves.

So we take the first step into our healing process by acknowledging the fear and the shame that stem from our wounds. As we become more conscious of our shadow material, we see how we project it onto others. We put the problem out there in the world, where we cannot solve it no matter how many locks we put on our doors or alarm systems we install.

The problem is not an external one. Even though others may have wounded us or betrayed us, the hurt is being carried inside. The walls that must be taken down have been erected within our own minds and hearts.

This gets a bit tricky, because it is not our fault that someone attacked or betrayed us in the past. As a child we did not know when a situation or a person was dangerous. And often abuse happened because our parents or other caretakers were not protecting us sufficiently. So we did not cause the abuse but we experienced it and at some level we are still carrying the pain and the shame of it around with us. And, on a deep unconscious level, we blame ourselves for what happened, even though it was not our fault.

As adults we need to learn to take ourselves off the hook. We need to forgive ourselves for what happened to us and learn to bring love to the child within who was traumatized. This takes time and deep emotional work.

If we stay with our healing process long enough we create a deep bond with the child within and we make a commitment to love and protect that child in the future. We re-parent ourselves. We become the protective and responsible parents that we did not have growing up. So now it becomes our responsibility to create safety for the child. And, as we said, as we create safety, trust can gradually be restored.

You have heard the expression "trust but verify." We are saying something similar. We are saying "feel safe first and then trust will come gradually over time." Feeling safe is going to involve investigating and getting to know the person and situation. We don't walk into the room until we know that the room is reasonably safe.

Trust issues for severely abused people can take one of two very different forms. The obvious one—the one we have already mentioned—is inability to trust. But the other one that occurs is "inappropriate trust." This means that we continue to trust people we have no business trusting and constantly re-create our wounds.

The urgent need in this situation is to create boundaries with others so that we can stop attracting abusers into our lives. We cannot begin our emotional healing work if we are still stuck in a vicious cycle of abuse. We need to protect ourselves from people who would injure or control us. And we sometimes need to ask for help in order to extricate ourselves from an abusive situation.

So you can see that lack of trust is a universal issue. All of us need to learn to trust more, but we must start where trust begins, in our own hearts. Our initial challenge is to forgive and trust ourselves, and then to learn to set appropriate boundaries so that we feel safe with others.

Cultivating trust is a process that takes time and emotional courage. So we need to be patient and take baby steps. We cannot rush the process or force ourselves to trust before we are ready.

THE PRACTICE

Today, notice when you are not trusting others or yourself. Get in touch with the fear or shame that is making it difficult for you to trust and understand the wound behind it. How were you abandoned or betrayed in the past?

Your childhood wounds and the shame and the fear associated with them cause you to contract and freeze up emotionally. A red light comes on and the energy stops flowing in your life. In the desire to protect yourself you shrink back from opportunities that might benefit you.

When the red light comes on, you have to stop and pay attention. You can't force yourself to move forward if you don't feel safe, so focus on why you don't feel safe and ask yourself what you can say or do to create greater safety in the situation. By honoring the red light, you mitigate the danger, and you might find a way to move forward slowly. Or you might have to tell others that you feel scared or overwhelmed and you can't move forward now. You might have to tell them you need time and ask for their patience.

Today, when the red light comes on, take the pressure to move forward off the table. Stop, pause, breathe, tune in and take time to create safety. Understand that just because you don't feel safe now doesn't mean that you will never feel safe. There are just things that you may need to say or do in order to be ready to move though the fear or the shame that is coming up for you. Oftentimes, setting boundaries with others will create enough safety for you to move forward.

If your pattern is to trust inappropriately stop running the red lights. Something is compelling you to speed up and lose control. You may be ignoring or overruling your fear and that puts you in danger. Learn to feel your fear and make friends with it. Then you can slow down your reactive behavior and stop putting yourself blindly and repeatedly at risk.

Once you trust yourself to create safety, trust in others will come little by little. It will be an organic process. You will stop at the red light and move forward when the light turns green. You will stay out of dangerous situations and gravitate toward people and situations that are safer for you.

In time you will see the amazing results that occur when you feel safe enough to follow your heart and trust the universal energies moving through you. Things that used to be difficult to accomplish will happen easily and without great struggle or effort. Trust helps you live in the flow of the universe. You move with the flow of the river, instead of against it. Life becomes more spontaneous and joyful. Trust in yourself, in others and in the divine leads to a life of surrender and grace.

JOURNALING QUESTIONS

Where in your life do you need to create greater safety so that you can build trust with others?

Are there people in your life who are not trustworthy?

DAY 11

———

Optimism

Optimism is a state of consciousness. We cultivate optimism when we see things in the most positive light. Even when life seems grim, we do our best to find the silver lining. We look beyond appearances to see the wisdom and the truth that can be found in each experience. We keep hope alive even when things appear to be hopeless. If the glass is empty we know it will soon be filled up. Highs always follow lows. We just have to be patient. Without optimism, we see through a glass darkly, adding our own darkness and despair to the collective fear that is rising. Optimism helps us to keep our own consciousness free of judgment and fear and contributes to the health and well being of our people and our planet.

OPPOSITE STATES OF CONSCIOUSNESS: Pessimism, Negative thinking, Apocalypticism, Conspiracy theories, Hopelessness, Despair. When we realize that we are being negative and seeing life through a glass darkly, we need to realize that we may be making things worse and take the dark glasses off. Pessimism can poison our own consciousness and lead to depression and despair. Awareness of our negativity is essential if we are going to cultivate a spiritual vision for life.

THE TEACHING

Some feel the optimist is naïve, but this is not necessarily so. S/he does not have to be in denial of what is happening in order to see it in the most positive light. Plus, s/he knows that things are not always as they appear to be. Not only does the wolf appear in sheep's clothing, but sometimes the sheep can be mistaken for a wolf. It works both ways.

While the pessimist is running around spouting conspiracy theories and predicting the end of the world, the optimist knows that time often brings understanding and healing and even those who act with cruelty can make amends and find the way back to their hearts.

The optimist refuses to write people off or give up on them. S/he holds the space for healing and awakening. S/he does not deny that people make serious mistakes and fall from grace, but s/he believes in the power of forgiveness and holds the space for redemption.

While the pessimist says, "Things are bad and will only get worse," the optimist says, "Well, we will see about that.... The jury is still out and the verdict may surprise you." While the pessimist is always waiting for "the shoe to drop," the optimist is working happily without shoes. The pessimist focuses on what is lacking and complains endlessly about that, while the optimist focuses on what is already there and works to grow it and build on it.

When Jesus was told by his disciples, "We have only two fishes. How can we feed all these people?" Jesus demonstrated that what we have can be multiplied many times over if we accept it with gratitude and are willing to share.

If you tell me that I don't love you enough, you devalue the love that I give and it will not grow. But if you tell me you appreciate my love, especially when I am being difficult, my love will grow and become stronger.

I have said many times over. Tell me what you like, not what you do not like. Tell me what you want, not what you don't want. Focus on what is present, not on what is absent.

The optimist focuses on the love that is already there and so it grows and thrives. The pessimist says that love is not enough and his search for more love always comes up empty.

Optimism leads to gratitude for what we have and increases it. There is always more of a good thing. That is the key to abundance.

Pessimism leads to finding fault with what we have and gradually undermines it. That is the key to scarcity.

If you know that you have enough you do not worry about the future. You learn to trust and to surrender. You grease the wheel and it moves easier and faster. Knowing that you have enough inevitably leads to prosperity.

On the other hand, if you believe that you do not have enough, then you compromise what you have and eventually you have less of it. When you believe you don't have enough, you create having less. Lack inevitably creates more lack.

Knowing this you can begin to understand the price you are paying for being pessimistic. It not only decreases your joy and your capacity to love; it also decreases your bank account.

Many people talk about seeing the glass as half full. That might be helpful in the beginning to change the way you perceive things. But the deeper meaning will still elude you. What is the meaning and purpose of a glass after all? A glass is meant to help us drink. That is why it was created. It was not created to be empty.

Of course, after you drink the water or the wine, the glass will be empty. But that is just a temporary state. When the glass is low or empty it can be filled up again and continue to serve its purpose.

Like that glass, you were not created without a purpose. You were not created to be empty. You were created to be filled up by the power of love and to share that love with others. You were created to be an expression of love in this world.

Yes, there may be times when you feel empty, depressed, and without a purpose in your life. But that is just a temporary state. It tells you that it's time to re-align with the presence of love in your heart and fill your cup again.

To do that you have to change the way that you talk to yourself and others. You cannot afford to be negative. You can't continue to wear dark glasses and be pessimistic about yourself, other people or the world. You have to change the way you think and talk to yourself and others.

You have to learn to give up despair and to embrace hope. If you do, you may be amazed at the results. A hopeful person creates a life of joy and abundance—not overnight perhaps, but little by little. Each day the power of light increases until it consumes the darkness.

Your optimism is a lifeline back into the divine flow. It helps you move out of your dark, dreary cave into sunlight and blue skies. Instead of feeling sorry for yourself and remaining a victim, you begin to fulfill your purpose, sharing your joy, giving and receiving love. And all this happens because you change the way that you talk to yourself and to others.

THE PRACTICE

Today be aware of your negativity and pessimism. Understand that they have the power to degrade the quality of your life and do not identify with your negative thoughts about yourself, others and about the world you live in. Today, take off your dark glasses and see your experience in a positive light. Look for the silver lining. No matter how bad it seems, don't despair. Find hope and embrace it.

Much of what occurs in life is influenced by how we see things. Seeing in a negative way just makes things worse. And you don't want to do that. You want to make the situation better, not worse. So you must learn to bring light to the darkness. You must learn to bring love to your fear. You must bring hope to your despair.

You are the bringer of love to your own experience. You are the one who decides what everything means to you. Interpret events in a negative way and you reinforce that negativity. Interpret them in a positive way, and you awaken to their true purpose.

Today, focus on the meaning you give to everything

that happens. Do you make it good or bad, positive or negative? Do you see it as a punishment or a blessing? What is your interpretation?

If you interpret in a negative way, take a pause, and ask to see it differently. Ask yourself how you can be more hopeful and optimistic.

Do this throughout the day, one thought and feeling at a time. Be the witness to your state of consciousness. You are the judge and the jury. What is the verdict you give?

It may not be easy to learn to be optimistic if you have been a pessimist all your life, but you have to start somewhere. You have to change your self-talk, moment to moment.

As you do this practice throughout the day, be gentle with yourself. You are not going to do it perfectly. You will forget and fall into old patterns. That's okay. Just catch it as soon as you can and come back to your heart.

Changing only one out of ten of your negative interpretations can have significant results. And the more you practice, the more effective you will become.

JOURNALING QUESTIONS

What negative attitudes or interpretations of life do you need to transform?

Today were you able to be aware of your judgments and interpretations and just be present as a witness to what happened?

DAY 12

———

Perseverance

Perseverance is a state of consciousness. We cultivate perseverance when we are committed to our cause even when we face major resistance or obstacles. We refuse to be deterred or beaten back. We stand our ground. We stand up for what we believe to be true and right. Perseverance enables us to overcome prejudice, falsehood and deception. It helps us challenge injustice and be a thorn in the side of people and institutions that oppress others and deny their existential and constitutional rights.

OPPOSITE STATES OF CONSCIOUSNESS: Timidity, weakness, spinelessness, cowardice, giving up in the face of difficulty. When we find ourselves shrinking back or being intimidated by those who wield money, power or influence, it is time for us to take a stand for what we know and believe is fair and right.

THE TEACHING

Not everything that is true or right comes easily. Sometimes our freedoms must be fought for. Sometimes we are asked to resist what is wrong and stand up for what is right. This takes great courage and conviction. It may mean that we have to put ourselves in harm's way in order to protect and defend innocent people who are being abused by others.

Our collective perseverance led to the founding of our country, the abolition of slavery, and the granting of voting rights to women. We see great courage and perseverance in the allies standing up to Hitler, the struggles of the civil rights movement, and recent efforts of people advocating for gay rights and gender equality. As Ruth Bader Ginsberg points out, meaningful change happens one step at a time. It does not happen overnight. It is a long and difficult process that extends over the generations.

Perseverance means that we are steadfast and loyal to the people and principles that we care about. We don't shrink back when our rights are violated. We stand up for what we believe in. We refuse to be intimidated by money, power, or social pressures. We do what is right even when it is not convenient or popular. We take a stand even when others threaten or humiliate us.

Standing up against injustice takes courage and strength. We have to draw deeply from our inner spiritual resources. We cannot be weak or easily intimidated if we want to expose those who are abusing their power and privilege.

Courage and conviction are required not just in standing up for others, but also in standing up for ourselves. Most of us are not born with a silver spoon in our mouths. We have to work hard to be successful. We need to be steady when the ground shakes beneath us. We need to push through resistance and overcome obstacles. We need to believe in ourselves when others don't.

When unforeseen obstacles arise and things don't go our way, we must be steadfast and patient. We have to pull back from the abyss and wait until the time is right to move forward. When we really believe in something, we don't give up. We recalibrate, revise, and shuffle the deck till the right cards come into our hands. When they do, we play them without fear. We have the courage to be ourselves and to ask for what we want and deserve.

What is right does not always happen by taking the course of least resistance. Sometimes you have to take the wheel and steer the boat over the rapids. If you are afraid to step up and take responsibility, innocent lives can be lost. Witness what happened to the *Costa Concordia.*

When we persevere we maintain vigilance. We don't go to sleep on our watch. We take our responsibilities seriously. We show up every day and do the job we signed up for.

You can't be weak, sloppy or undisciplined and build a solid business or a happy family. Others have to know they can count on you. You need to know that you can show up even when it is challenging or difficult.

The weak cannot persevere in the face of difficulty. They shrink back, abandon their positions and allow them to be overrun by the enemy. At best, they are intimidated or overpowered. At worst, they are turncoats and traitors, who throw others under the bus in a shameless effort to save themselves.

To persevere you must stand up for yourself. You must stand up to protect those whom you love. You must stand up for fairness and justice. You must be committed to what you know is right, despite the odds against you.

THE PRACTICE

Today, practice standing up for yourself and others. Practice pushing through difficulties. When you can't push through, don't hit your head against a wall or a rock. But wait patiently and stand your ground. Be vigilant until you see the signs that darkness is lifting and dawn is breaking. Today, stay alert. Do not go to sleep on your watch.

Today, take responsibility when you are asked to. Don't wait for others to do it for you. Stand up and stand firm so that others can lean on you if they need to.

Don't give up on yourself or on others who depend on you. Don't abandon ship. Don't be a coward and shrink back or run away from difficulty.

Today, understand that success is measured not just by what comes easily to you, but also by the obstacles you struggle against and eventually overcome. A courageous woman or man is not afraid to fight for the people s/he loves or the principles s/he believes in.

Water is buoyant. Even a small river can float your boat and carry it downstream. Like water, you can live in the flow and lift others up. When possible, always move with the current of the river and not against it.

But water is also persistent. Its progress is not impeded by the obstacles that stand in its path. It always finds a way to flow around them and in time even those large trees limbs and boulders are worn down by the rushing water.

Today, be like the river. Take what comes your way and live gently in the flow of your life. When obstacles arise, move around them. Don't be impeded by the challenges that arise. Move forward in any way that you can.

When you believe in yourself, you have the patience to wait when it is necessary. You understand that all obstacles are temporary. The river always finds a way forward. Its progress cannot be denied.

JOURNALING QUESTION

Understanding that success is measured, not just by what comes easily to you, but also by the obstacles you struggle against and eventually overcome, when have you been committed to what you know is right despite the odds against you?

DAY 13

———

Faith

Faith is a state of consciousness. We cultivate faith when we trust in the basic goodness of human beings and the universe in which we live. Even when bad things happen, when other human beings disappoint or betray us, we don't give up our hope and optimism. Even when we live through a natural disaster or another catastrophic event, we don't blame God or believe we are being punished. We know from deep within that we are loved and blessed and we trust that, even when we don't understand what is happening right now, in time God's plan will be revealed to us. Our faith enables us to weather the times of crisis in our lives and to emerge safely from the fire and fury around us.

OPPOSITE STATES OF CONSCIOUSNESS: Lack of faith, Despair, Inability to find purpose and meaning for our lives, Lack of emotional resilience due a disconnection from our Core Self, Distrust and inability to perceive goodness in ourselves, others and the universe in which we live. Our myopic vision and self-absorption make it difficult for us to see the big picture or to feel that a higher power or a force for the good is active in our lives. When our vision narrows and we can't see the forest for the trees, it is time to climb to higher ground so that we have a longer and wider view. It is time to get out of our heads and into our hearts, where we can connect with love and regain our faith.

THE TEACHING

Like Job in the Old Testament, we are all tested at times by events and circumstances that feel overwhelming to us. At such times we are challenged to reconnect to the source of love within in our hearts and to find our faith.

Many of us feel defined from the outside. So that when something bad or difficult happens to us, we think that we are somehow to blame and are being punished by God or by other human beings. We condemn ourselves or we condemn others for what happened. This closes down our hearts and makes it difficult for us to recover from adversity or trauma.

If we are lucky, in time we take ourselves and others off the hook and find a renewed sense of meaning and purpose for our lives. We may even understand in retrospect why the event or circumstance had to happen, in order for us to wake up and pay attention to our soul's need for growth.

And then we know that it was not a punishment, but a blessing.

Many times—if not indeed all the time—we don't understand what is happening or why it is happening, so we try to give our own meaning to it. We interpret what happens either positively or negatively, and either interpretation can be erroneous.

If we are wise, we withhold judgment and try to accept and live with what is happening until we better understand it and can respond in a helpful way. We learn to say, "I don't know why this happened and I don't know what it means." We take time to try to get our arms around it so that eventually we can embrace it and work with it. As we take this necessary time, we hold ourselves and others harmless. We do not blame or shame anyone.

Job was a master at living in his heart and having faith in himself and his God. When calamity after calamity was visited upon him, he refused to blame God. He always looked within and asked, "What is God teaching me or asking from me?" No matter what whirlwind was whipping around him, he stayed deeply in his center and refused to be caught up in the external drama. He never doubted that God loved him.

Because Job never doubted the goodness of God that goodness was finally revealed to him. He was tested many times, but he never lost his faith and in the end his faith was rewarded. That is why, as it says in the 23rd Psalm of King David, "Goodness and Mercy follow him all the days of his life and he dwells in the house of the Lord forever."

Job models for us how to stay anchored in love and truth no matter what seems to be happening around us. All of us have our "Job moment," a time when our faith is tested. What is yours? How has your faith been tested in the past? How is it being tested right now?

THE PRACTICE

Today, see if you can be with your experience without interpreting it. Just be with it and try to get your arms around it. It is okay if you don't understand what is happening or why it is happening.

Today, be open to the possibility that whatever is happening in your life might be happening for the good, even if you don't see where that goodness abides. When difficulties arise and you feel overwhelmed, be willing to see the lesson you are being asked to learn.

Most negative events and circumstances arise from our own karma. They are the inevitable consequence of our thoughts, feelings, beliefs and patterns of behavior. Sooner or later, our chickens come home to roost and we have to deal with it. We have to take responsibility for what we have created.

That doesn't mean that the universe is punishing us. It just means that It is awakening us to the need to make different choices in our lives. It is asking us to change our consciousness so that we can change our experience. When we take responsibility and learn our lessons, we plant better seeds that will grow into healthier plants. We always reap what we sow.

Today, ask yourself, "Am I blaming God or the Universe for the difficulties or obstacles that I am facing?" If the answer is "Yes," be a little more restrained and humble.

God does not want to punish you. God just wants you to wake up and take responsibility for what you are creating.

Today understand that life always challenges us to deepen our understanding and our faith. That is why we are tested. That is why there are lessons for us to learn along the way.

Remember something important here. God tests you because he loves you and wants you to grow. He does not ask you to learn something that you are not able and ready to learn. You just have to be willing to learn and you will pass the test.

During challenging times we either trust God or we don't. If we do, that trust will see us through and we will cross the threshold. If we don't we will shrink back into victim consciousness and the door will not open to us.

JOURNALING QUESTIONS

What is your "Job moment?"

How has your faith been tested in the past?

How is it being tested right now?

DAY 14

———

Gratitude

Gratitude is a state of consciousness. We cultivate gratitude when we feel grateful for the gift of life and appreciate all the good things that people do for us. We do not take what we have for granted, but value all the ways that the universe supports us and insures that our needs are met. Gratitude leads to abundance.

OPPOSITE STATES OF CONSCIOUSNESS: Lack of gratitude, greed, wanting more, feeling that we do not have enough, focusing on what is missing instead of what we have, poverty consciousness, bitterness or jealousy toward others who have more than we do. Lack of appreciation keeps scarcity alive.

Without gratitude it is impossible to experience abundance, even if you are rich in money and possessions. When you lack gratitude, you don't feel blessed by what you have and so you do not enjoy it. You are preoccupied with holding onto it and protecting it from others who have less, or you are always trying to get more because you don't believe that you have enough.

Being rich and feeling abundant are not the same thing. In fact, you can be poor and experience great gratitude for what you have, be willing to share it with others, and know that the universe always meet your needs, one way or another. Such a person is rich in spirit. His gratitude and willingness to share with others creates the conditions in which the resources he needs flow back to him. He hardly ever feels lack because his most important needs are being met in any given moment.

Jesus told us that it is easier for a camel to fit through the eye of a needle than it is for a rich man to enter heaven. That is because the rich man is attached to his possessions. He is storing up riches that he cannot take with him when he dies.

Holding onto our possessions means that we have a miserly state of consciousness. A miser may have a lot of money, but he lives a miserable life.

When we feel gratitude for what we have, it is easier for us to be generous and share with others. We put our resources to work in the world. We use them to reach out, engage, employ or support others. We create a flow of energy that eventually returns to us.

Gratitude keeps the flow of abundance going. It creates connection and reciprocity. It enables us to celebrate life together. On the other hand, lack of gratitude leads to lack of joy, lack of trust, lack of energy and lack of prosperity.

In order to feel gratitude we must value the gift. If you don't have any money and haven't eaten in three days and I give you five dollars, you will no doubt be grateful. But if you inherited hundreds of thousands of dollars from your father, and I buy you lunch, you might not be very thankful or impressed. The key to feeling gratitude is valuing the gift. If you don't value the gift you won't be grateful. And that means that you will still be living in scarcity consciousness even though your net worth is thousands of times more than mine.

There is an expression that "what comes around goes around," but that cannot happen if you don't value the gift and share it with others. If you are grateful you will share the gift and it will benefit others as well as yourself. Then it will also be true that "what goes around, comes around." This is the cycle of abundance.

Here are the simple steps:

1. Value the gift.
2. Give thanks for the gift. Express appreciation.
3. Share the gift with others. Pay it forward.

Practice these three steps and you will be amazed at the results.

All of us were given the gift of life by God and our parents. Do you know and appreciate the fact that your life itself is a gift? If you know this, you will feel grateful for what you have been given and try to live a meaningful life. If you don't realize that you have been given a gift, you may squander your life. You may become a victim feeling sorry for yourself and resenting others. You might fall into crime, poverty or addiction; you might even attempt suicide.

If you do not value your life, you probably won't value the lives of others. You won't express gratitude toward your partner, your parents or your children. You will take all of this for granted. And then one day, they might be taken from you and you will be shocked at the size of the hole in your heart.

Don't wait for tragedy to happen to tell them how much you care about them and appreciate the gifts that they have given you. Do it now.

THE PRACTICE

Today, take time to value the gifts that you have been given and go out of your way to say thank you for to the people who love you and support you. Don't take anyone for granted. Don't diminish any gift that is offered to you, no matter how small and insignificant it may seem. Take time to notice all the affection, caring, courtesy, praise, support, compassion, and understanding that is offered to you. And say thank you. Say, "I noticed how supportive you have been to me and I want you to know that it means a lot to me!"

And then take the time to pay it forward. Offer support to someone else who is struggling. Share the gift so that it can be extended and increased in kind. Today, be a force for love in the world by telling others how much they mean to you. Acknowledge, value, and express appreciation for all the good things in your life.

Expressing gratitude is prayer in action. Thanking God for his blessings and his bounty every day helps you stay connected to your higher power and aware of its presence in your life.

Today notice when it is hard for you to value the gift or express appreciation for it. Be aware of the times when you feel envious or jealous of others. Observe when you feel that you do not have enough and are looking for more.

Question yourself when you think you lack something. Ask yourself, "What do I have that I am not grateful for? What gift am I taking for granted? How can I appreciate what I have if I am always finding fault with it or believing that it is not enough?"

Today, recognize the signs that you are living in victim consciousness. Every time you complain, find fault, see or experience lack, remember that your lesson today is about gratitude. Even if you cannot be grateful, be aware when you are not and try to understand what block to love is lodged in you heart.

Today do not be a miser. Do not hoard or withhold resources from others. Be generous. Offer a blessing or an alm, extend a hand to others. Give gladly without thought of return. You are blessed to be in a position to share or to help so take advantage of the opportunity.

JOURNALING QUESTIONS

When have you valued the gifts you have been given, expressed appreciation for them and shared them with others?

How can you do that right now in your life?

DAY 15

———

Tolerance

Tolerance is a state of consciousness. We cultivate tolerance when we accept the differences between us and respect each person's background and experience. People often have differing racial, cultural or religious backgrounds. They often have different political beliefs or personality traits. While we usually feel safer when we are around people who look and talk like us, we are all challenged to open our hearts and minds to people who don't fit that mold.

OPPOSITE STATES OF CONSCIOUSNESS: Intolerance, prejudice, narrow-mindedness, racism/sexism/homophobia, lack of acceptance or condemnation of others who are different from us.

THE TEACHING

Most of us feel very insecure about who we are. That's why we like to travel in a pack where everyone conforms to the same social norms. That way we don't stand out and don't invite inspection or criticism. Only those who do not belong to the pack are scrutinized, distrusted and often ostracized or condemned. Cults, gangs, fraternities, extremist or terrorist groups are characterized by rigid conformity to a set of beliefs and behaviors that make the group members "holy and right" and everyone else "unholy and wrong."

Fundamentalist religious and political groups do not easily accept people who hold different ideas or beliefs. They are threatened by differences and may even attack, slander or seek to humiliate people who disagree with them.

The irony is that real love is not based on agreement. It is easy to accept and support people who agree with you. But real love means being able to accept others who don't agree or have a different tradition or experience. Real love only happens when we accept and tolerate differences.

Real love embraces the individual as s/he is, whatever s/he believes and whatever s/he looks like. It is always challenging to love people unconditionally. We have to be very secure about who we are to love without conditions.

As soon as the individual joins a group that espouses a set of exclusive beliefs his ability to love unconditionally is significantly compromised. To meet another person face to face, he must surrender the beliefs that separate and divide him from others.

People in many fringe groups will engage in abusive words they would not speak and actions that they would not take if speaking or acting alone. The group provides cover. It gives them license to commit crimes and rationalize their offenses.

Only when the individual is separated from the group can he see what he has done and take responsibility for it. Pedophile priests are protected by the church. Klansmen hide their faces under white hoods. Until that protection is shattered and the white hoods are removed, crimes remain hidden and undetected.

Fortunately now the victims of crimes—previously isolated and bought off by their abusers—are coming forward. For them too, there is safety in numbers. Once one person has the courage to stand up for herself, the others follow. Once the serial abuser is finally exposed, even the group cannot protect him.

Each individual is responsible for his thoughts, feelings words and actions. He cannot hide behind his family, his church, his political party or his company. In order for justice to be done, all forms of cover must be removed so that each individual is held to account for his actions.

Prejudice and intolerance can be institutionalized. They can become a tool used by a country, a political party or a religious institution to keep their base happy and their opponents at bay.

However, we must remember that all of this starts in the hearts and minds of each individual. My prejudice and yours feeds the collective appetite to prop ourselves up at the expense of others.

So we must come back to our own deep insecurity that makes it so very hard for us to accept or tolerate others who are different from us. We need to see how often we are triggered each day. We need to see how we look for similarity and agreement with others and are challenged when we do not find it.

Just as love is not based on agreement, our well-being as a people is not measured by how alike we are, but on how well we accept and integrate our differences. When we make our peace with living in a pluralistic society characterized by differences in race, religion, gender and other forms of identity, all of us thrive. One person or group does not benefit at the expense of others.

THE PRACTICE

Today be aware when you feel threatened by someone who looks different from you or has a different belief or experience. Remember that love is based on acceptance, not on agreement. Today, practice accepting others as they are. Understand that there is room for everyone to have their own beliefs and experiences. You do not have to convert others to your point of view. By respecting others, you make acceptance possible, even when agreement is lacking.

Today practice good boundaries. Accept your experience and let others have their own experience. Know that what works for you does not necessarily work for others, and vice versa.

No matter how wise you are, you do not know what works best for others. You cannot understand where they have been or what they need. You have to trust that they know what works for them and give them the freedom and the respect they deserve.

Today focus on inclusion, not exclusion. Invite people into a shared space but allow them to have their own experience and to express their own ideas. Do not dominate the discussion, but create a safe space where all voices can be heard.

Today be mindful of your prejudices and the beliefs that separate you from others and create unnecessary conflict. See if you can put yourself in their place and walk in their shoes. See if you can view others as equals.

Make space for acceptance and understanding within your own consciousness. Be willing to surrender old biases and judgments that you blindly accepted because they were drilled into you by parents, teachers or religious leaders. You don't have to hold onto beliefs that have become destructive or dysfunctional.

Today let go of narrow mindedness and divisive beliefs. Create a larger, more inclusive and convivial space that is respectful to everyone. Today, find common ground and let the differences be what they are. Today be an equal. Don't see yourself as "better than" or "less than" others.

When you tolerate others who are different from you and respect their freedom of speech and other constitutional rights, you establish equality and insure that justice is done impartially. You help to create a safer world.

JOURNALING QUESTIONS

What differences between you and others trigger you?

How can you accept and respect others even when you do not agree with them?

Courage

Courage is a state of consciousness. We cultivate courage when we step forward to protect others. We do not cower in the shadows and hide from danger to save ourselves, but we lead the charge and meet any threat to our safety or freedom head on. Parents protect their children, first responders put themselves in harm's way to save the lives of others. We spontaneously step forward when others need our help, even if we put our own lives at risk. When we consistently exhibit courage, others look to us for direction and leadership.

OPPOSITE STATES OF CONSCIOUSNESS: Cowardice, Weakness, Timidity, Avoidance of responsibility, Making excuses or running away when our help is needed, Betraying or abandoning others.

Few of us are born with courage. It is something we cultivate as we develop self-confidence and learn to meet the
challenges of our lives. Even a small person can be brave.
David was just a child when he stepped forward and slew
Goliath. Of course, it is easier to be courageous if you are
strong and confident. But even a strong person like Goliath
can be defeated if he is over-confident and underestimates
the strength or skill of his adversary.

Courage is born in the face of danger or adversity. We
might be afraid—indeed we might be trembling in our
boots—but we take a deep breath and move though our
fear. We show up even when it is scary.

If courage required lack of fear, no one would be courageous. We can be afraid and still be willing to show up. We
can answer the call even if we don't know how we will succeed. The person who runs into a burning building to save
a child does not know how he will do it or whether he will
be successful. He does not deliberate. He just acts spontaneously. He answers the call and hopes for the best.

Some of the most courageous people are unlikely
heroes. They aren't people who have great powers or proven
track records. They are people who were in the right place
at the right time and they were willing to say and do what
they could. They were instruments of divine grace. When
push came to shove, they refused to bow down or go to the
back of the bus.

Don't think you are too small, too weak, too awkward or
too insignificant to be brave. More than anything else courage takes willingness. If you are willing, God can use you.

If you are not willing, no amount of strength will serve you or anyone else. You can go to the gym and work out 5 hours a day and still run away when you see three guys assaulting a jogger in the park.

Courageous people do not live just to serve their egos or save their own skins. They care about people. They protect their families, but also serve their communities. They reach out to protect those who cannot protect themselves. They help to lift people up who have fallen. They rescue others from danger.

In a topsy-turvy world, the weak serve the strong. The poor get poorer and the rich get richer. But in a world where hope is kept alive and justice is served, it is the strong who serve the weak and the rich who serve the poor.

Fortunately, a few outstanding corporate billionaires like Warren Buffett and Bill Gates had epiphanies and rearranged their priorities. They were also unlikely heroes. Now they lead in a different way than they did before.

Courageous men and women provide moral leadership. They are role models and show us how to stand up for ourselves and others.

THE PRACTICE

Today, be aware when you are asked to stand up for yourself or for others. Even if you find it scary, step into the opportunity. Hold your fear gently and walk through it. In order to develop courage, you must be willing to be seen and heard. You can't hug the wall or disappear into the corner. You have to get out on the dancefloor.

You don't have to know how to dance. You know how to

walk. That is enough. Walk to the center of the room, bend your knees and wiggle your butt. Be willing to make a fool out of yourself and you won't fail. The worse thing that will happen is that people will laugh. If so, laugh with them.

After you have been out on that floor once, it will be easier to do it next time. Only you will know all the walls you had to break through to let yourself be seen and heard. Only you will know what a "fraidy cat" you were.

When you learn to speak up for yourself, it becomes easier for you to stand up for others. Gradually, you begin to trust that your job is to walk through the door when it opens to you. As a result, you will learn to take risks and open yourself to new experiences. You will leave behind your self-protective shell—the prison of your own making—and jump into the river of life. And in time you will be seen and heard in ways you never thought possible before.

Your self-empowerment happens because you stopped hugging the walls and walked through your fear. Be grateful to the universe for giving you a kick in the derriere. The first step is always the most difficult.

Today have the courage to take the first step and the next one will follow. You don't have to rush. Take your time, but don't stop. Keep moving, one step at a time.

Today, be courageous. Walk through your fear. And then give yourself credit. You deserve it!

JOURNALING QUESTION

When have you walked through your fear and stood up to protect yourself and others?

DAY 17

———

Integrity

Integrity is a state of consciousness. We cultivate integrity when we remain true to our values and keep our commitments. Our behavior is consistent for it stems from an inner coherence. The left hand knows what the right hand is doing. We have made an integration of different aspects of our personality with the resulting wholeness. The spiritual adult is holding hands with the wounded child. High and low, light and dark, left and right hemispheres are connected. We don't make promises that we can't keep or act in an ambivalent way with others. People feel that we are present for them and that they can rely on us to do what we say we are going to do.

OPPOSITE STATES OF CONSCIOUSNESS: Lack of integrity, Inner conflict and incoherence in the psyche lead to ambivalent or contradictory behavior. Flip flopping, frequent changing of mind, bi-polar mood swings result. There is a split in the psyche in which different aspects of personality compete for prominence and control, resulting in inconsistent words and actions, swings of energy and attention. People cannot rely on us. They never know which one of us is going to show up. Will it be the light side or the dark side, the spiritual adult or the wounded child?

THE TEACHING

All of us have a major piece of healing to do in this life. We need to integrate persona and shadow, light and dark, spiritual adult and wounded child. Accepting one aspect of self—the one we like—and denying or projecting the other—the one we don't like—reinforces the polar split within the psyche. The left hand says and does one thing, while the right hand says and does the opposite. Lack of coherence within results in ambivalence, inconsistency and unreliability without.

We say that someone has integrity when we feel we can rely on that person. S/he has a consistent moral compass, tells the truth and keeps commitments. S/he does not make promises s/he cannot keep or speak out of both sides of her mouth. When s/he is wrong, s/he admits it and apologizes.

A person without integrity can be a bullshit artist, a sociopath, or a serial liar. You cannot trust such a person and you must learn to set boundaries and keep your distance. Sometimes this person's insensitive and inconsistent behavior is not intentional. It simply results from a deep split within their consciousness. Until there is healing and integration in the psyche they will be a landmine going off under your feet when you least expect it.

Some of this inner split in the psyche is reinforced by social norms and expectations. We are told that there are only two types of people is this world: good people and evil ones. Of course, we want to be the former, so we go out of our way to deny and project our shadow energies.

The problem with this strategy is that it does not acknowledge the fact that everyone has a shadow and a persona. Even the so called "light bringers" have a dark side and a flicker of light can be found in every soul, no matter how deeply it has lost its way. The challenge we all have is to integrate the polarities within the psyche. This creates an inner connection, an energetic flow between the poles in which extremes are harmonized. This is the essence of the healing journey. It results in wholeness, or integrity.

Without establishing coherence within, all outward behavior will be inconsistent or ambivalent at best and schizophrenic or sociopathic at worst. What we call goodness does not come from a denial of the shadow but from an integration of it. The more we deny or bury the shadow in the depths of unconsciousness the stronger and more unpredictable it comes.

And then we wonder why someone jumps off a bridge or shoots innocent people from a hotel room window. Both are walking time bombs, but most of us do not hear the ticking in their chest when they walk past us.

When we know the importance of psychological healing and integration, we make it the most important job we have to do. Parents, teachers, coaches, clergy, and even peers must have an ear to hear the muted screams of the walking wounded. We need to learn to reach out to them before it is too late.

Only when people think there is something wrong with them that cannot be fixed, when they feel that love and acceptance will never come do they jump from the cliff. We need to find them and reel them back into the family and the community before they reach the edge. And we need to get a safety net in place for those we cannot stop from trying to take their own lives or someone else's.

Those who are not mortally wounded will find themselves in prison or back on the street. What chance do they have to heal? What opportunity will they have to see the light within and integrate their dark side?

When the prison door opens and the street swallows them up, will they have wholeness and integrity? Or will they be driven from within by the same inner conflicts that resulted in their old criminal or anti-social behavior?

If you have taken the time to heal your own wounds, you know that the support of a community of caring people is essential for the healing process to take place. You cannot heal if you don't have a safe place to be.

So who will bring the safety net for the next terrorist or school shooter in the making? Who will see the signs and get him the help and support he needs?

To have integrity means we have created cohesion and harmony within our own consciousness. We have taken the time to be nurtured by love and acceptance, to forgive ourselves and others, and to take responsibility for our lives step by step. This is what brings peace and wholeness to our hearts and to our world.

Today, be aware when you are out of integrity. That means that your words and actions are not consistent. You are not walking your talk. You are not being honest and transparent. You are being ambivalent with others and so they don't feel safe. They don't know where they stand with you.

Today, tune into the conflict within your own psyche that is fueling this kind of inconsistent or deceptive behavior. Ask yourself, "Why am I afraid to tell the truth? Why is shame or fear coming up for me?"

Today, realize that anything that you say or do when you are being triggered by shame or fear will be destructive to yourself or others. So hold your tongue and tie up your horses. Don't project your internal conflict outward onto others. Take some time to breathe, to look within, and to see what needs to be healed within your own mind and heart.

Integrity cannot be cultivated if you are being dishonest with yourself or others. You must give up the bullshit. You must stop trying to fake it, hoping you are going to make it. Even if you make it, you aren't going to make it better. You will only make it worse.

Integrity comes from within. You must make peace in your heart before you can take any positive action. Have the courage to look at your fears, your feelings of insecurity, your anger, your mood swings, your contradictory thoughts. Take an inventory of the contents of your consciousness and try to get your arms around all of it. Don't try to push the negative thoughts and feelings away. Acknowledge everything that is there. Sit with all of it and embrace it. That's the first step: being honest and transparent with yourself.

Once you have done that you can say something truthful to others and do something that is consistent with that truth. You can speak and act with integrity. You can say for example: "I can see that I am being ambivalent. I go back and forth between wanting the relationship and wanting to be free. I can see how I desire you, and also how I get scared and try to push you away. I know this isn't what you might like to hear, but this is what is going on. I don't want to lie to you or lead you on."

When you tell the truth you take a lot of pressure off yourself. After all, it isn't easy being a bullshit artist and pretending to be something you are not. It isn't easy disappointing people all the time. Truth can help you take off that mask and be seen as you really are. You can stop faking it and be more authentic.

That can be the first step in connecting you to your heart and moving your relationships with others to more solid ground. But it requires a time of introspection. It means you have to look for truth within and stop keeping the outer charade going.

Today, take a pause. Let the play have an intermission. When the outer play stops, your "inner mission" begins. You take time to come into your heart and get in touch with what you really think and feel. You can separate the wheat from the chaff, the truth from the lies. You can take your costume off and dance in front of the mirror.

JOURNALING QUESTIONS

When in your life have you shown the most integrity?
When in your life have you shown the least integrity?

DAY 18

———

Equality

Equality is a state of consciousness. We cultivate equality when we see each person we meet as an equal brother or sister. That means that we do don't feel better than others and look down on them, nor do we feel inferior and put others up on a pedestal. Each person has the same existential worth and deserves the same rights and respect that we do. In order to cultivate equality we must overcome our own shame so that we do not project it onto others. When we see others as guilty or "less worthy," we are betraying our own guilt and unworthiness. We see in others only what we believe about ourselves. We are mirrors for one another.

OPPOSITE STATES OF CONSCIOUSNESS: Inequality, feeling "greater than" or "less than" others. Judging or despising some and worshipping others, believing that some people are better or more spiritual than others, or that some people will be saved and others will suffer in hell. When there is lack of equality there is injustice. We objectify others and rationalize our attempts to attack, condemn or oppress them. People are brutalized and crimes are committed in the name or God or country.

THE TEACHING

When we are little, our parents are so much bigger and stronger than us, it seems they have all of the power and they can use it to control us. They can beat us or withhold love from us when we are bad or uncooperative and there's not much we can do about it. So we learn very early to behave in a way that meets with their approval.

Later on, we may become the victim and attract parental figures into our lives who dominate or victimize us. Or we may become just like our parents and victimize others. The seeds of inequality are sown early on in life and sprout and bear fruit in adulthood. The whole thing is a set up.

So we can't really talk about equality without talking about inequality. In our world, some people are strong and others weak. Some are rich and others poor. Some are educated and others not. Some are victimizers and others victims.

Except in a few rare cases, we do not experience equality so much as we do inequality. Granted those times when we were really treated as an equal and afforded dignity and mutual respect are life-changing. When we are loved and appreciated as we are, we are inspired to love back. We understand that equality is the goal that we must strive for, even though our experience consistently runs shy of it.

Jefferson wrote in the Declaration of Independence, "All men are created equal, (and are) endowed by their Creator with certain unalienable rights." Yet as we know, Jefferson himself was a keeper of slaves, and they were not equal nor were they endowed with the right to "liberty and the pursuit of happiness." It took 90 years for slavery to be abolished and 190 years for some of these rights to be realized during the civil rights movement. Still, today, in spite of the progress, we do not have equality in the United States of America, or anywhere else in the world.

Equality is a goal we aspire to, but it will always be "the promised land" until the promise is fulfilled. We can and must continue to struggle for equal rights for all, but we also know the real struggle is not out there in the world. It is right here in our hearts. Until we walk through our shame and cease to blame others, equality cannot get a foothold in the world of form.

That is why we must focus on all the ways in which we do not feel equal to others. We must look at why we feel inferior or superior, why we victimize others or allow ourselves to become victims. There are childhood wounds, erroneous beliefs and reactive behavior patterns that must be faced. Until we heal the wounded child within, s/he will never stand as an equal with any of her brothers and sisters.

How can you win the war against poverty if you carry poverty in your consciousness? How can you win the struggle for equal rights if you yourself do not believe you are equal? How can you stand with your brother or sister if your heart is not open?

The seeds of inequality have been sown within our consciousness and it is there that they must be uprooted so that the seeds of equality and justice can be planted. As long as you and I carry prejudice in our hearts and minds justice cannot be done in this world.

The world, after all, is just a reflection of who we all are. What we carry in our hearts and minds will eventually out-picture in the world.

THE PRACTICE

Realize today that when you feel "less than" or "greater than" someone else you are encountering your own shame and unworthiness. You aren't unique in this. We are all carrying fear and shame from childhood. Our shadow has been lurking within, unseen and unheard, although we have been projecting it out into the world non-stop.

Today, do not project the fear and shame, but see them and hold them compassionately. See that the judgment you would make about another person is but a reflection of how you feel about yourself. See that the person you would attack or condemn is a mirror for you.

When you bring awareness to your shame and your prejudice you see that you withhold love and acceptance from others only because you feel unworthy of love yourself. When you bring love to the child within who feels unlovable, you can take others off the hook. The more you fill up on love, the less need you will have to judge or attack others.

Existentially all of us are equal. What you want and

what others want is the same. You want to be respected and treated with dignity. You want to be accepted and loved. The other person wants the same, even if his skin is a different color or he has a different name for God. You both have "inalienable rights." When these are rights are mutually honored and respected, you and he can live in peace.

There are karmic laws at work in this world. What comes around goes around. What you grant to others will come back to you in the end. When you know this, how can you entertain a single prejudicial thought? How can you judge or attack anyone?

The decision to project fear and shame, to judge and attack others, comes from within your own consciousness. If you connect to love and bring love to the child within who feels unworthy, then you will not project your shadow. Instead you will own it and integrate it. You will feel more connected to others and you will bring understanding and compassion, instead of blame and shame.

Today, take a few baby steps forward on the road to equality. For what you believe in your mind and nurture in your heart will find its way into manifestation. As within, so without. As with you, so with others.

JOURNALING QUESTIONS

When have you experienced the most equality with others?

When have you experienced the least equality with others?

Do you understand that people who trigger you are mirroring back to you aspects of yourself you have not yet learned to love?

DAY 19

Creativity

Creativity is a state of consciousness. We cultivate creativity when we suspend our routines and automatic patterns of thinking and try new approaches to solving the problems and challenges of life. Sometimes our lives become too predictable and there is no room for growth and transformation. We need to switch off the cruise control or the automatic pilot so that we can respond spontaneously to opportunities that arise. When the old energy field around us is no longer held in place by habitual patterns of thinking, new doors open and we can walk through them. This enables us to be more playful and engage in activities that bring greater joy to ourselves and others.

OPPOSITE STATES OF CONSCIOUSNESS: Living on automatic pilot, habitual or rote behavior and patterns of thinking, being stuck in unhealthy energetic patterns that emphasize duty and sacrifice over joy and spontaneity. Our routines are inflexible, our roles rigid, and our time highly pressured or conscribed, sabotaging our energy so that we are unable to take risks and grow beyond our fear-based limits.

THE TEACHING

Creativity brings new energy into our lives. Old patterns and routines fall apart and new directions are explored. Like a child with a new toy, we investigate all the possibilities and have fun doing it. Joy and playfulness are the characteristics of living a creative life.

In our world, energy moves into form and expresses through that form. But no form lasts forever. Every form has a useable life. When its lifespan is exceeded the form either explodes or implodes. When energy expands from within and the form is unable to expand to contain it, the form will explode. Energy will be liberated and it will find a new form to inhabit or a new way to express. On the other hand, when the form contracts and the energy inside it is compressed it implodes. In other words, it collapses into itself or disintegrates from within. In this way also, the energy is disembodied and has to find a new way to express.

In spiritual terms, this is the cyclical process of life, death and rebirth. In Physics the same principle is explained by the first Law of Thermodynamics, also known as Law of Conservation of Energy. This law states that energy can neither be created nor destroyed; it can only be transformed or transferred from one form to another.

Cycles are part of life. Forms come into being and then fall apart. Then the energy that is liberated finds a new form or way of expressing. When we are conscious of our cycles and cooperate with them, rebirth becomes both a conscious act and an organic process. We detach from the old willingly and so create the space for the new energy to come in. The form does not need to explode or implode (a violent act) for it is surrendered gracefully.

It is one of the challenges of life that old forms must die for energy to be transformed and reinvested. This is how life renews itself. The creative energy cannot manifest until the space is created for it to express. So either there is a let go and a detachment from old energy patterns or there is an explosion/implosion that releases the energy.

From a practical point of new, you foster creativity by letting go of old rigid patterns of thought and behavior. If you cannot let go, you set yourself up for a more dramatic event, in which you are forced to let go. In the Hindu tradition, this is the Shiva energy taking over, coming in to destroy the old so that the new can be born. For us the question really is how to cooperate with Shiva so that the old can be released without major trauma.

The death of form results in a period of chaos or formlessness. The energy swings are intense and frequent until the energy released finds a new form or a direction for its expression. This is true, albeit to a lesser degree, even if we cooperate and voluntarily detach and let go. Exploration and playfulness are the first part of the creative process.

That is why creative energy cannot and should not be

embodied or invested in form before it is ready. It needs time for exploration. The beginning of a cycle is not the time for commitment, structure or discipline. That is why I point out in my book *Having the Time of Your Life,* there are two years of detachment (8, 9) and two years of exploration (1-2) in any given 9-year cycle. Only years 3-7 are moving concretely into form. They are the five active years of the cycle.

The lesson here is that we often put so much pressure on ourselves to succeed that we just keep re-creating the same limiting forms in our lives. We do not grow, because we have not expanded beyond our limited beliefs and habitual behavior patterns. The more we restrict our growth and keep old energetic patterns alive, the more frustrated our soul becomes, because the goal of the soul is growth and transformation.

If we don't learn to detach from rigid forms and roles, fixed ideas, and dysfunctional energetic patterns that result in self-betrayal, then our soul will cry out for Shiva's help and we will go through a big drama. The earth will shake under our feet. A volcano or tidal wave of emotion will erupt.

THE PRACTICE

Today, be open to new, creative approaches to life. Let go of fixed thinking, rigid roles and repetitive or habitual behavior patterns. Try a new diet, find a different way to drive to work, turn off the television and take a walk on the beach.

Today try to see the world as if you are looking at it for the first time. There is a huge part of life you are not experiencing because you keep looking at it from the same angle. Today, open your eyes a little wider. See the big picture or change your perspective.

You are most creative when you allow yourself to explore and to play. So don't be afraid to daydream or brainstorm. Write down your thoughts without editing yourself. Just let the words come tumbling out however they want to. You are not writing for anyone else. You are not trying to impress anyone.

Today, dance like no one is watching. Give yourself the freedom to be and to explore. Don't try to be practical. Don't try to write your business plan or make big commitments/decisions. It's not the time for that. So take the pressure off. If you can, take the day off from work. Or at least change your daily routine. You don't have to perform today. Just have fun. Just walk through the open doors and see where they lead.

Notice when you are putting the pressure back on yourself. Observe when you are trying to fit into a structure that no longer works. Be mindful when you are taking yourself or others too seriously. Can you just relax and have fun? Can you enjoy the process without knowing where it is going to lead?

Creative artists in any genre learn to trust their intuition. Art is not a rational or intellectual process. It is a play of the mind and the heart. It is an exploration into uncharted waters. If you know where it is leading, chances are it is not art. It is something else.

If a new idea comes in, dance with it. Don't try to understand it or qualify it. Just bring it in. And let the next one come in right after it. Stream of consciousness is the human form of the universal play.

There will be time later to edit or create structure if that is what is needed. But if you bring the structure in too soon, you will squeeze out all of the creative energy. Today is a day to expand, travel, learn, play, explore. It is not a day to create form.

The creative energy will eventually find the form that suits it. But not today. Today, we don't know what it is or where it is going. Today it is in free flow.

Tomorrow it might become a sonnet or Haiku, but today it is just free verse. It is not sight reading the notes in the score. There is no score. Today is a day for improvisation.

We don't know where we are going and we don't need to know. Isn't that in and of itself an amazing gift? That is the gift that creativity brings to all of us.

JOURNALING QUESTIONS

When have you been most creative in your life?

How can you be more creative right now?

DAY 20

———

Peace

Peace is a state of consciousness. We cultivate peace when we stay in our hearts and connect with our Core Self. We do not get lost in the drama of life with its push and pull, attack and defense, blame and shame. By resting in our hearts we avoid unnecessary struggle and contention with others. When fear arises and we feel anxious, we know that we have moved up into our heads and it is time to re-center. So we refrain from saying or doing anything that will intensify our fear or that of others, and we focus on connecting with the love in our hearts.

OPPOSITE STATES OF CONSCIOUSNESS: Inner conflict, contention with others, trying to manipulate or control when it is time to submit and let go. We lose our peace when we identify with fear-driven thoughts and emotions or with ego agendas that put pressure on ourselves and others. When this happens, we need to get out of our heads and back into our hearts. Then, we can re-connect with love and trust in the flow of life.

THE TEACHING

We cultivate peace when we stop resisting life and fighting unnecessary battles. Like moving water, we find a way to flow over or around obstacles. We go where we can when we can. We do not try to beat down walls that are stronger than we are. We are not contentious. We aren't looking for a fight. Our goal is not to live in opposition to any person or idea, but to find a way to transcend personality traits and belief systems.

When others contend or rage, we find the place of quiet within. We settle in and settle down to the place of peace where the heart is calm and the mind is open. That is true tranquility, like the surface of a lake on a clear day when only gentle breezes stir the water.

We submit and surrender to the energetic flow of life. When the lake flows down into the river, we move with the current, knowing that to swim against it will be ineffective and will only exhaust us. When we come to a fork in the river we change direction without great difficulty.

Life brings us opportunities in the right time and place. We do not have to make them happen. Pushing the river does not make it flow where we want it to. It is a waste of time and energy. Indeed, all ego agendas are ineffective and futile. They create tension and striving. Stress builds up within and frustration grows without.

Better to let go of the need to stand above or apart from others. Better to merge into the stream of life. Living in fear and self-preservation leads only to self-destruction and conflict with others. There is no end to this.

That is because our ego expectations can never be satisfied. As soon as one need is met, another one arises. That is the endless drama of life when we live and react in fear, when we are always looking for "more" because we don't feel we are enough.

To be serene, we must know that we are enough. Nothing is lacking. No pieces of the puzzle are missing. At worst, they are just temporarily misplaced and we will find them when we relax and stop looking. To be serene, we must trust the universe and have faith in its inherent goodness. Without trust and faith, it is impossible to surrender.

Self-importance and the need to control are obstacles to peace. If we really want peace, we need to stop taking ourselves so seriously and learn to accept that at any given moment God may have a better plan than we do. Yes, humility helps, and so does patience, because the timetable of the divine plan may not match up with our expectations.

Our perfectionism also must go. We must be okay with being an ordinary human being who makes mistakes and we must be okay with the imperfection of others. To expect ourselves or others to be perfect is a recipe for crucifixion. Do we really want to go down that road? Or are we willing to be more gentle with ourselves and others?

To put it another way, the only thing that is not perfect is this life is our need to be perfect. When we don't need to be perfect any more, one of the major obstacles to peace is removed.

All this comes down to understanding our true place in the universe. We are one facet in a many-faceted jewel. We are not the only one who shines. All facets shine together. All beings are wedded together in a great symphony of life.

If we know that Spirit is in charge and not our egos, then surrender is possible. We can learn to hold our fear gently so that we do not live in reaction to it, causing all kinds of mayhem around us. Holding our fear gently helps to quiet us down so that we can reconnect with love. And once we are connected to love, we can find our way back into the flow of life.

Perhaps the most important journey we take in this life is the one from the head to the heart. Yet we focus on taking a different journey, seeking the holy grail out there in the world where we continue to meet resistance and we struggle to survive, often at the expense of others. Even when we try to help, we end up interfering adversely in the lives of others. As hard as we try we cannot fix others. Indeed, the fixer himself is the obstacle to peace.

Neither the Seeker not the Fixer succeeds in the end. Both are worn down by the struggle. They return home exhausted, depressed, without hope or faith. While they set out on what they thought was a God-inspired journey, they return home dispirited, bitter and angry at God.

As we know, it is not easy for the Don Quixotes of this world to admit defeat, to acknowledge that their romantic quest was egotistical and doomed to fail. It is not easy to come to terms with the fact that the Grail cannot be found in the world, no matter how far we travel or how diligently we look for it.

In the end we came back to the place where we began. We have to take a few deep breaths and bring ourselves back into our hearts. That is where the Grail is found, not in some far distant place or time, but right here and right now, breath by breath, thought by thought.

We like to think that some of us are more advanced than others and so we can take short cuts to the mountain-top. But sooner or later we find out that every shortcut we take ends in a cul de sac. What we thought would save time only extends the time necessary to take the journey.

It becomes yet another experience of false pride, another lesson in humility. And so we return to Beginner's Mind. We are all beginners. We all start from the same place, over and over again.

If you are not patient you cannot be at peace. *A Course and Miracles* says only "infinite patience brings immediate results." Is your patience infinite? If not, you might have to wait in line for a while. And, in the end, you may realize that what you desired and asked for is not what you really want or need.

THE PRACTICE

Today, when you are anxious or disturbed about anything, practice breathing and coming into your heart. Slow things down. Let everything be as it is and be gentle with yourself and others. Nothing is worth losing your peace over. Your peace is more important than all of the ups and downs of your ego agenda.

Today, surrender your ego expectations and connect to love so that you can understand and align with your spiritual purpose. Stop trying to manipulate and control, stop trying to be perfect or to demand that others be perfect. Your ego needs are misguided and will only bring suffering to yourself and others.

Today, you need to go deeper. You need to take the journey to your heart and connect with love. Then you will come back into the universal flow. Bring love to the child who does not feel worthy of love. Give him support, encouragement and hope. He does not have to jump through hoops to get love and acceptance. You can give it to him right now.

Bring love and peace will follow spontaneously. And, of course, the contrary is also true. Withhold love and there will be no peace in your heart or in the world.

Today understand that your spiritual work is not out there in the world. That is not where the holy grail will be found. Your spiritual work is done within your own consciousness. Clear your mind and open your heart. Breathe and be. Sink into your Core Self.

That is where you are connected to the Source of Love. Once you are connected, you will be a beacon of peace and an instrument of love. You won't have to make anything happen, because it will all happen effortlessly through you. You will be an open vessel, a conduit for divine love and purpose.

Of course, you can only do this if you are willing to surrender your little will to the Greater Will. If you are afraid of God and think He will punish you if you make a mistake, you cannot be a conduit for love. Love cannot flow through a contracted heart. It needs a heart that opens and stays open.

Today ask yourself throughout the day, "Is my heart open?" If the answer if "No," then realize it is time to acknowledge your fear and hold it gently until it settles down and your heart opens again. If the answer is "Yes," then you know you have found the place of safety and tranquility within and the peace of God abides with you.

JOURNALING QUESTION

Where are you at war in your life and how can you come back to peace?

DAY 21

———

Fidelity

Fidelity is a state of consciousness. We cultivate fidelity when we are faithful to the people we love and to the values and ideals we hold dear. Fidelity requires consistency and discipline in thought and emotion. We value and respect those people and principles on an ongoing basis. We may be tempted to betray others by offers of money, status or sex, but we resist the temptations and remain true to our commitments.

OPPOSITE STATES OF CONSCIOUSNESS: Infidelity, Betrayal or abandonment of people and ideals we have committed to, Lack of emotional allegiance, Promiscuity, Inability to remain true to ourselves or others, Erratic behavior patterns that undermine the trust that others have for us.

Good relationships are built on trust and emotional allegiance. Only when we feel that someone has our back and will be there consistently for us do we fully open our hearts. That is why infidelity often takes a mortal toll on a relationship. When our trust has been betrayed by someone it is hard to trust that person again.

As Jesus pointed out, it is possible to be faithful to someone in deed, but unfaithful in heart or mind. We can lust after a man or woman who is not our partner and still remain physically faithful. But is that real fidelity? Is divided or partial loyalty true loyalty?

In an ideal soulmate relationship, or spiritual marriage, there is mutual fidelity of body, heart and mind. There are no caveats, conditions or exceptions. Temptations might arise from time to time, but they cannot gain a foothold. The commitment of each person to the other endures and strengthens over time.

In such a relationship equality reigns. The needs of the partner are respected and considered to be as important as one's own needs. Each person consistently asks not just, "What is good for me?" but also, "What is good for my partner?" And both people ask, "What helps our relationship to grow and thrive?"

This is the ideal we strive for, but we do not always achieve it, so we must learn to see where we are being selfish in the relationship. Where are we being insensitive or oblivious to what our partner needs? Or where are we neglecting our own needs just to make our partner happy?

The more aware we become of the inequalities, the more important it becomes to speak up. Learning to speak and listen from the heart is essential if we wish to move into greater intimacy and trust.

Without good communication, we move apart and live in our separate worlds. Intimacy suffers or disappears. Trust is slowly undermined.

How can you be faithful if you do not trust your partner and s/he does not trust you? It just is not possible. Sooner or later, thoughts become actions and infidelity of one kind or the other occurs.

Don't wait for a crisis like that to happen. Watch for the signs of separation that are precursors of infidelity and start communicating in a heart-felt way. Get the help of a therapist if you can. The only way to save a speeding train on the wrong tracks is to slow it down before it reaches the cliff.

It is also helpful to remember the relationship between fidelity to self and fidelity to others. Fidelity to self means that you are committed to your own interests, values and purpose in life. That keeps you on track and makes it possible for you to enter a relationship as a whole person. Fidelity to self means you have cultivated integrity. You know who you are, what you want, and what you can commit to.

When both people are faithful to themselves they have a much greater likelihood of being faithful to each other. They join together in strength rather than in weakness. They do not look to the other person to complete them or make them happy. They avoid co-dependent patterns that result in stagnation and prevent growth in the relationship.

Today, be aware of when you are faithful to yourself and when you are not. Also notice when you are faithful to your partner and the other important people in your life, and when you are not.

Today, be cognizant of when you live up to your ideals and commitments and when you don't. Notice when you compromise your values or are tempted to betray yourself or someone else.

Today, ask yourself, "Am I trustworthy? Does my partner trust me? Do I trust her or him? Are we able to communicate in a heart-felt way so that we put our cards on the table and we know where we stand with each other?"

Today, look at your relationship honestly, and consider whether you are being faithful to it physically, mentally, emotionally and spiritually. Is your sexuality engaged in a healthy way or do you find yourself watching porn or feeling attracted to other potential partners? Is your heart engaged? Are you emotionally open to each other or are you growing apart? Is your mind engaged? Can you discuss and share ideas without arguing or making each other wrong? Is your spirit engaged? Is there a higher sense of purpose and direction that you both share?

Look at each area (body, heart, mind and spirit) and rate the relationship on a scale from 1-10, with ten being the highest. Have your partner do the same if s/he is willing. The highest score is 40. What is your score? What is your partner's score? A score of less than 20 from either one of you suggests a relationship in crisis or heading there.

Don't use this exercise as a club to beat yourself or your

partner. Use it as an invitation to honest dialog and a call for help, if you are willing to ask for it.

Fidelity is not something that comes ready-made. It is something that develops as each person individuates and as intimacy and trust are established in a relationship. These are the building blocks. Are you and your partner committed to building the foundation?

Fidelity is an issue not just in marriages/partnerships but also in friendships, relationships with parents and children, relationships at work and in our places of worship. When we are faithful, we are loyal and committed to the people we care about and that loyalty and commitment are what insure the strength of our families and communities.

Today consider how loyal and committed you are to the people who love you, support you and share your life. Today, seize any opportunity that arises to deepen your trustworthiness and demonstrate your loyalty to the people and principles you love.

JOURNALING QUESTIONS

What issues of fidelity or infidelity have come up in your life?

How can you be more faithful to yourself and the people you love?

DAY 22

———

Moderation

Moderation is a state of consciousness. We cultivate moderation when we avoid extremes in thoughts, feelings or actions. A moderate person is not driven by uncontrollable urges, phobias, fetishes, obsessions, or addictions. S/he does not give credence to conspiracy theories, rigid or authoritarian ideas, or extreme religious or political beliefs. S/he seeks to find a balance is all areas of life. S/he does not live on the edges of life but seeks the middle, invites compromise and cooperation and tries to find common ground.

OPPOSITE STATES OF CONSCIOUSNESS: Immoderation, extreme ideas or beliefs, uncontrollable feelings, addictive or obsessive actions. A person who lacks moderation may experience bi-polar swings of emotion, and various types of phobias or obsessions. S/he may exhibit grandiosity, megalomania, narcissism, sado-masochism, and other personality disorders. S/he may be drawn to cults or fringe groups that demand obedience to some cause or charismatic leader. A person who lacks moderation is emotionally unstable and lacks an ability to center and find balance in life.

THE TEACHING

Many of us believe that more is better. But sometimes more money, more sex, more food, more booze, more surfing the internet can be addictive and ultimately unsatisfying. In order for us to regain our health and equilibrium less may better than more. When we consume less we do so out of the awareness that our consumption has been out of control and we have to get a handle on it. We need to establish healthy limits for ourselves.

On the other hand, having less than we need is not healthy either. If we don't have enough money or food or sex we can feel deprived and we can be driven to seek more at any cost. This crosses boundaries that should not be crossed.

Having too much and too little are unhealthy. It is far better to have "just enough" for our needs to be met. That way we take nothing for granted and stay aware and alert to potential addictions.

When we live in moderation, we do not consume too little or too much. We take what we need and give any excess back to others. We find balance and harmony in our lives and do not fall prey to the physical diseases and psychological maladies associated with under or over-consumption.

Moderation is also important when it comes to our ideas and beliefs. A moderate person knows that every coin has two sides and avoids one-sided approaches because they lack balance and fairness.

A moderate person listens to both sides of the argument and then decides. Where possible, s/he tries to find areas of common ground. When disagreements exist, s/he ties to find ways for both sides to compromise. In all of this there is a trust in dialog and negotiation, a sense that both parties have some insight to contribute and that the best decisions are made when both sides of an issue are heard.

In all fields of life—in politics, religion, and social life —moderation is the key to creating balance and inclusion. There is room for everyone to have their own perspective and beliefs as long as they respect the beliefs and perspectives of others.

Seeing both sides of the coin, hearing both sides of the argument, does not require agreement, but it does require mutual respect. We can disagree with others without questioning their integrity or attacking them personally.

People who lack moderation often cross boundaries and attack people who have different beliefs or cultural perspectives. They blame, shame, and slander others because they feel threatened by differences. They do not understand that the freedoms and the rights they would take away from others will one day be taken from them if their attacks succeed.

The inability to accept differences in race, religion,

culture, gender and other forms of physical or social identity leads to totalitarian governments that restrict freedoms, and undermine or suppress human rights. You can see this happening across the globe.

On the individual level, any extreme idea or obsessive emotion creates fear and lack of safety for others. That is why we all need to take responsibility for our thoughts, feelings, and actions. No one else is responsible for what we say or do. If the words that come out of our mouths are hateful, if our actions are harmful to others, we need to understand that we are out of control and get help before it is too late.

If we have addictive behaviors and abuse drugs, alcohol, food, or other substances we may destroy our health and alienate the people we love. If we are rage-aholics or are physically abusive, we might hurt someone we love. Or if we are silent and tolerate abuse from our partner we might get seriously hurt or put our children at risk.

Before we go off the deep end and lose control, or allow someone else to melt down, we need to get help, call up a friend or a 12-step sponsor, dial 911 or a help hotline, find a therapist or enter a treatment program.

If our ideas are inflated or delusional, if our moods swing back and forth between excitement and depression, if we have various fixations or phobias, are often angry, overwhelmed or agitated, we might need to go to a doctor who can prescribe medication that will help us tone things down.

If we are members of a cult or an authoritarian group that engages in brainwashing, mind-control, or social intimidation, we might need reach out to a family member, a former cult member, or a law enforcement officer to get help extricating ourselves from the group.

If we believe in conspiracy theories, engage in hate speech or are drawn to para-military or terrorist groups, we are in crisis and headed for the proverbial cliff. We need emergency assistance. If we know someone who is in this situation, we need to consider making some kind of intervention.

The goal is always to stabilize and to regain balance in our lives. Extremes in our thinking and our emotions are not healthy and create a volatile energy in our consciousness. At any point the energy can go over the edge, create a schism or rift in the psyche, in which we dissociate and do something harmful to ourselves or others.

THE PRACTICE

Today, notice when you are consuming too little or too much. If you have too little, ask for a little more. If you have too much, reduce your portions.

Today be mindful of any extreme ideas or feelings that are coming up for you. Notice any fixed ideas, phobias, obsessions or patterns of addiction. Notice any strong swings of emotion, especially anger/rage or suicidal feelings. Notice when you feel overwhelmed or anxious about something. What do you do or say when these emotions come up?

Today, pay attention when the ground shakes for you and the volcano of emotion is about to erupt. Can you tell when you are ready to go over the edge and say or do something that will be hurtful to yourself or others? Can you pause and breathe? Can you find a way to regain your balance?

Today be mindful of any strong ideas or beliefs that you have in which you are convinced that you are right and others are wrong. Can you allow another point of view without feeling angry or threatened? Can you see both sides of the coin, not just the one you called when the coin was flipped?

Even if you are right today, you may be wrong tomorrow. Sometimes you call tails and heads comes up. Are you a good sport or a sore loser? Are you going to shame or attack others because they have a different experience or perspective from you?

Can you see and accept differences, even though you are not in agreement with others? Can you make space for everyone's voice to be heard? Can you be inclusive, instead of exclusive?

Today, understand that free speech is an ideal that we aspire to, but we cannot reach our goal if we do not understand the ways in which we prevent the voices of others from being heard. When you see yourself standing in the way of someone else's freedom of expression, be aware that you are trespassing and step out of the way. For the freedom you give is the freedom you will receive.

There is something in our lives that is more important than agreement. It is acceptance. With acceptance, everyone can be heard, not just the ones who share our experience or point of view.

When we insist on agreement, rights are violated and freedoms undermined. Fascism wins over democracy.

Of course, we love it when we agree. We love having our ideas and beliefs supported by others. We might even believe that support equates to love. But it is not so. Love is not based on agreement. It is based on acceptance and mutual respect.

When we insist on agreement, we never find a middle ground. Extremes dominate. Intolerance prevails. Conflict continues in our hearts and in our world.

It is time for us as a society to let go of the tyranny of agreement and let acceptance and tolerance of differences be the foundation of our discourse. Then we will not objectify/dehumanize each other or seek to justify our trespasses.

When we build our foundation on acceptance, moderation is the rule. Moderation helps us find integration in our consciousness, and health and well-being in our bodies and minds. It helps us find balance and harmony in our family and our community. It helps us to tolerate differences, find common ground and experience equality in our interactions with each other.

JOURNALING QUESTIONS

Where do you need to bring moderation into your life?

In which ways do you have/consume too much or too little?

DAY 23

———

Ecstasy

Ecstasy is a state of consciousness. We cultivate ecstasy when our hearts are open and we allow ourselves to be infused and supported by the energy of unconditional love. We move beyond our ego needs and our struggle for survival into a psychological state of transcendence in which we trust the universe to support us and guide our activities. We joyfully and willing answer the call for love without fear and so become an empty vessel through which the divine can reach to earth. As love flows through us our hearts go on fire, our spirit rises up and we radiate light to all around us.

OPPOSITE STATES OF CONSCIOUSNESS: Solemnity, Brooding, Gloominess, Heaviness, Density, Depression, Lack of trust. In this state, we are preoccupied with meeting survival needs, the mind is anxious and defensive, the heart is distrustful and we begin to shut down emotionally. Energy does not flow in our bodies, muscles begin to contract, movement becomes painful and limited. Without faith in something larger than us, we are dispirited and do not have the will to care for ourselves or to engage in a healthy way with others.

THE TEACHING

When we are ecstatic we experience bliss, radiance, and joy. We may have epiphanies and revelations. We live a truly inspired life. This can happen only because our hearts and minds are open and trusting. We open our arms to receive love and we give it in return without deliberation.

Doors open for us without struggle and we move through them gratefully and gracefully. There is great spontaneity operating in our lives, so that we do not have to spend a lot of time planning for or controlling what happens. We know that our job is not to figure out why something is happening, but to show up to the best of our ability and do our little part in the divine plan.

Living a joyful, ecstatic life means we express our creativity and engage in work and relationships that nurture and challenge us. We are not drawn to any form of self-repression and we do not work or relate to others out of sacrifice or duty. We give others the same freedom to express themselves creatively and do not seek to control, confine or repress them.

Some might call this a win-win approach to life. You win because I can be myself around you. And I win because you can be your authentic self with me. My joy feeds you and yours feeds me. Each of us encourages the other to self-actualize.

An ecstatic life has a strong spiritual component. We feel that there is a higher power operating in life and it is guiding us to serve the greater good. We don't need to get credit for our contribution because the real credit goes to the One who guides us and supports us.

If we were running an ego-agenda, seeking name, fame, or credit for our words and actions, we would get in the way of the divine energy and it would ramp down. Doors would cease to open before us and we might become anxious and frustrated. When that happens—and it does even for people who can embody ecstatic energy—we have to realize that we have bought into our fear and lost our trust. We have pushed the angels away and tried to take charge with our egos. Of course, that never works.

So we have to remind ourselves that we are not here to do our ego's bidding or to be driven by our fears. We are here to serve the divine purpose and we can do that only when our hearts and minds are open. We need to reestablish trust and be worthy of the trust that is placed in us.

Living an ecstatic life requires that we set time aside for communion with God and connection to our spiritual community. This helps us to keep our hearts open.

When we get too busy and preoccupied with the affairs of the world, our attention moves from the heart back up into the head and our connection to love becomes attenuated. We have to return our attention to our heart and reconnect with love if we want to re-establish the flow of grace and purpose in our lives.

THE PRACTICE

Throughout the day today, be aware of when your heart and mind are open and when they are not. When you are open and receptive you can receive love and share it with others. It is a very natural thing. You don't have to look for love. It is already there. You just have to open your heart to it and then giving and receiving happen spontaneously.

When you trust, the energy flows and the doors open. When you lack trust, the energy ramps down and the doors begin to close. Today, notice this as it occurs in your consciousness and experience.

Today, try not to say or do things out of duty or sacrifice. Move joyfully toward your creative expression. Be playful and open. When you do what you love to do and find most meaningful, you are living in an inspired way. What you are devoted to and stay present with will continue to grow and prosper. The energy will build and much will be accomplished without great effort.

Today, remember to take baby steps. Take one step at a time on the flat stones in the river and you will cross to the other side. Don't try to cross the river by jumping off the cliff. Grandiose actions are wound-driven and make it clear that your ego has tried to take change.

When you are content to take one small step at a time, spirit supports you on your journey. It does not matter if you don't know exactly where you are going or how you are going to get there. You just need to know what the next step is. Then you can stay in your heart and make steady progress.

If you don't need God to do it with you, then you are living with false pride and you will pay the price sooner or later. The river carries many broken bones from people who were impatient and made reckless decisions.

Stop trying to push the river or swim against the tide. You won't make it. You will be a casualty of your own pride. Slow down and get centered. Let go and let God. Take one step at a time and let Spirit get behind you.

JOURNALING QUESTIONS

What has been your greatest experience of ecstasy?

How can you continue to be emotionally present and open to the ecstatic moment as it unfolds in your life?

DAY 24

———

Nurturing

Nurturing is a state of consciousness. We cultivate nurturing when we care for others who need our support. This may be our children, our parents, the poor, the elderly, the handicapped, or those with life threatening illnesses. Nurturing others is an expression of the Divine Mother energy of unconditional love, acceptance, and support. Even in the animal kingdom, mothers put the needs of their offspring above their own needs. They feed their children and protect them from predators. They are gentle with their offspring, but fierce with those who would hurt them or compromise their safety.

OPPOSITE STATES OF CONSCIOUSNESS: Not nurturing, Selfishness, Putting our own needs in front of those of our children or others who are vulnerable and need our support and protection. Being emotionally distant, and unable to express caring or affection, Abandoning or betraying those we have a responsibility to love and protect.

THE TEACHING

Nurturing is the primary attribute of the Divine Mother Energy. Mother cares for her children above all else and will even sacrifice herself to protect them or save their lives. Her love is unconditional and steadfast. There is never a time when she puts her own needs above the needs of the vulnerable ones she is here to support and protect.

All of us embody the Mother energy to some degree. We all have the capacity to nurture others. We do this by creating a safe environment in which others can grow and thrive. We learn to set healthy boundaries to prevent that safety from being compromised.

In the womb the child is nurtured and protected by the woman's body. Even when the baby is born, that nurturing and protection continue. The child needs a safe place to explore the world. It needs someone who pays close attention to it and is committed to meeting its needs.

When the mother's love is strong and committed the child thrives. When the mother is ill, incompetent or preoccupied with meeting her own needs, the child's needs are neglected. Abandonment or betrayal can result, leaving lasting trauma.

Of course, those who are incapable of nurturing others were very likely neglected or abandoned by their own mothers. They did not have a safe place to grow up in and so they do not know how to create safety for themselves or their children. In addition, boundaries may have been absent or insufficient and they may have been abused by strangers or other family members.

One of the great lessons of becoming parents is that we always re-create on some level the neglect or abuse we experienced in our own childhood. Or we may seek to compensate for our childhood experience by going to the other extreme. So if we were not protected as children, we may be over-protective of our own children. This results in a different type of wounding.

Ideally, we are nurtured and protected in healthy ways. We are given what we need, not more or less. That enables us to grow up and move gradually toward independence. When we are given too much mothering, we become co-dependent and have trouble individuating. On the other hand, when we are given too little nurturing, we individuate too soon before our physical and emotional needs have been met.

Being a good mother is not as easy as some might think. Before having children, we may bask in the romantic glow, but the process of giving birth and caring for a baby 24/7 brings us back to reality pretty quickly.

This brings up the important question, "How can we nurture others if we ourselves have not received healthy mothering, and never learned how to nurture ourselves?" The answer, of course, is we can't. We have to learn how to do it.

Self-nurturing is necessary if we are going to learn how to nurture others. We have to learn how to create a safe environment for ourselves, how to set boundaries with people we can't trust, how to commune with the little boy or girl inside who never grew up.

We have to become the loving and accepting mommy we did not have. We have to show up for ourselves, learn to meet our own needs, and give ourselves the caring and affection that were missing from our childhood. Obviously, this is a huge task and it cannot be accomplished overnight. It is the work of many years of healing and reconciliation. Right now, we have to be content to take the first few baby steps.

THE PRACTICE

Today, be aware of your mommy wound and see how it makes it difficult for you to give and receive love. Use every opportunity today to open your heart and bring unconditional love to yourself and others.

Today notice when you are creating safety for yourself and others and when you are not. As soon as you realize that you do not feel safe, stop what you are saying or doing. Take a time out to nurture yourself, to bring love to your inner child, and to set boundaries with others. Say, "I am feeling overwhelmed right now. I need to take some time for myself." Go for a walk in the woods or on the beach. Or just go to your bedroom, close the door, and give yourself some love.

When you see that others who are weak or vulnerable are being bullied or shamed by others, speak up and support them. When you see that others have needs you can meet, offer your help and encouragement. When your love is needed give it gladly.

Today be the nurturing mommy to yourself and to others. Understand that your love can make a huge difference in the lives of others. A simple hug or a few words of encouragement can change the course of someone's day. And it will have a ripple effect, touching others. That is because love is the greatest power in the universe and when it is given unconditionally, without strings attached, it has the power to lift up those who have fallen, and to redeem those who feel judged or betrayed.

Today, be the voice of Divine Mother who loves all of her children, without exception. Be her hands reaching out to those who need support, encouragement, or protection. And bring that love, not just to others, but to yourself, as well. For all beings are worthy of love. And if you do not take time to receive love, you will not able to bring that love forward into the world.

JOURNALING QUESTIONS

Where do you need to bring more nurturing to yourself or to others?

Are you able to embrace the nurturing that is offered to you?

DAY 25

———

Wisdom

Wisdom is a state of consciousness. We cultivate wisdom when we study and internalize the teachings of the great sages of the past and apply them to the challenges of today. We also deepen our spiritual understanding by learning the lessons that have come to us in our lives. To be wise is not just to be smart. It is to understand the inner nature of things, to look beyond appearances, to expose falsehood and discern truth, to discriminate between illusion and reality.

OPPOSITE STATES OF CONSCIOUSNESS: Naivety, Gullibility, Foolishness, Superficiality, Lack of discernment, Being swayed by appearances or popular beliefs and not looking at the underlying truth, Holding narrow opinions, Prejudice, Mindlessness, Stupidity, Irrationality, Having delusions or hallucinations, Inability to distinguish truth from falsehood.

THE TEACHING

Wisdom is not something that automatically comes with intelligence or a high IQ. You can be smart and not wise. In fact smart people who lack wisdom create a lot of problems for themselves and others.

Wisdom involves an ability to see into the inner nature of things, to look beyond appearances, beyond popular belief or opinion. A person cannot become wise until he has overcome his prejudice, bias and narrow beliefs. He must put his own opinions aside and inquire objectively into the nature of things. He must keep an open mind and be willing to learn something new. He must be willing to be surprised, baffled and challenged as he travels the path to truth, for there are many twists and turns on the journey.

Like a good baseball player, a wise person does not just hit a fastball. He learns to hit a curve ball, a slider and whatever else is thrown his way. He must be flexible and stay alert. Any fixed ideas that he has about himself, other people or the universe will be his Achilles' heel.

A wise person is not in a hurry to pin things down. S/he allows things to unfold. S/he knows that truth does not always reveal itself right away. You have to be patient and study things. You have to be vigilant and learn to see the patterns that reveal themselves. Only then do you begin to see what is really going on.

A wise person seeks the truth. S/he is not attached to any idea or hypothesis. S/he knows that attachment to certain ways of thinking and perceiving only narrow her vision and prevent her from seeing the truth. That means s/he must constantly let go of bias and preconceptions. S/he must refrain from making up her mind. S/he must remain open.

If s/he is invested in any particular result, s/he will be operating with blinders on. So s/he practices non-attachment, or mindfulness. S/he seeks to be the observer or the witness. She refuses to identify with or reject what she sees, but rather strives to remain neutral. Of course, this is a very difficult thing to do and s/he is not always successful.

As Einstein pointed out, the observer invariably influences what is observed. Subjectivity is inevitable, but practicing non-identification helps a wise person keep her own prejudice or preferences to a minimum.

While it is impossible to be totally objective, objectivity is the ideal that we must strive for in the quest for truth. Extremely subjectivity is likely to lead to delusions, hallucinations, and other forms of insanity. When we believe that everything that we think, feel or see is the only truth, we are unable to see the forest for the trees. We become lost in our own private world and disconnected from reality.

A wise person knows that we must overcome the filters within our own consciousness to see things clearly. That requires a daily spiritual practice in which we become aware of our constant ego-expectations, judgments and false beliefs. We need to become conscious of the dark glasses we are wearing and learn to take them off. As the good Book says, "First we see through a glass darkly, and then face to face."

If you are in a hurry to find the truth, you will just spin around in your own limited orbit. Wisdom requires patience. We must pierce through the pasteboard mask, we must remove falsehood one idea and bias at a time. To get to the truth, we have to uncover and expose illusions. Inner biases must go. And so must outer identifications. Until we stop marching to the drumbeat of popular bias and belief, there will be many demons holding onto our apron-strings.

Being a wise person means casting off inner and outer demons. Any person or idea we have identified with out of fear must be unmasked and repudiated.

Let us remember that the biggest blocks to wisdom are our own narrow ideas, prejudices and limited beliefs. If we are willing to become aware of them and question then, we will begin the process of unpeeling the onion skins of illusion that shroud the truth.

A wise person does his inner work. He works diligently to remove his filters. He also studies the powerful words of the wise teachers in the great traditions. The words of Jesus, Buddha, Lao Tzu, Krishna, Moses, Rumi and many others help him to understand universal spiritual principles that can guide his life. The teachings of these sages are as important today as they ever were. Indeed, they may be more important today, as we increasingly become disconnected from the wisdom of the past.

THE PRACTICE

Today, practice having an open mind and an open heart. Notice anything that comes up that narrows your mind or disturbs your heart. Everyone has a preconception or a bias. Everyone gets scared. What are your filters and inner blocks to the truth?

None of us like to admit that we have prejudices, fixed ideas, or blind beliefs, but we all do. If we cannot see these filters in our consciousness, then we are not able to perceive reality clearly. We see what we want to see. We see what is consistent with what we believe. And this is rarely the truth. At best it is one aspect of the truth. It is the tail of the elephant or the trunk, but not both.

Wisdom comes as you see and remove your own filters. It requires a committed spiritual practice of looking at your thoughts and feelings, understanding when you are triggered and fear or shame distort your perception. That is your spiritual work for today.

Today, do not pretend to know the truth. You may have an opinion but understand that is just an opinion among other opinions. Your opinions and perceptions are not the truth. The are the veil that separates you from the truth.

Today, practice discernment. Separate the wheat from the chaff. See your opinions, perceptions, expectations, biases, etc. for what they are. Set them aside. Remove the veil and see what lies behind it. Then we you will get closer to the truth. Then you will clear out some of the clutter in your mind so that you can see more accurately.

An authentic spiritual practice is not so much about finding truth somewhere out there in the world. It is about removing the blocks to truth within your own consciousness. When the obstacles are removed, when the veil is lifted, when your mind is clear and your heart is open, truth is right there. It abides in you and with you.

Today, peel back the skin of the onion, remove what separates you from the clear and calm center within. Today, clear your mind of unnecessary thoughts. Sink into a deeper and more profound level of consciousness. There you know what is true, even if you cannot put it into words.

That is okay. Sometimes words are not necessary and it is enough just to know the truth without speaking or acting on it. The time for words and actions will come when you are ready. Today, rest in the truth. There is nothing else that you need to do.

Today, be respectful of the ideas and opinions of others, even if they are different from your own. Invite them into discussion and dialog. Truth is inclusive, never exclusive.

A wise person understands that Truth is never given only to one person or to a chosen few. It is given to all of us. We just need to open our hearts and minds. That is the doorway. It takes a great modesty and humility on our part to cross the threshold.

Today, don't pretend to know when you don't. Don't seek to parade your wisdom seeking praise and approval from others. Be humble and restrained. Be vigilant for the blocks to truth in your own consciousness and seize every opportunity to surrender your opinions, prejudices and biases so that you can find wisdom in your heart of hearts.

Even though it does not feed your ego or improve your status in the world, abide with the truth and let it become your guide and your compass.

Today, let this be your practice. It is through devotion to practice that humble men and women of the past became great spiritual teachers. Today, in their names, and in the name of the most High, may you find and abide with the wisdom in your heart.

JOURNALING QUESTION

What biases, prejudices, preconceived notions or fixed ideas prevent you from seeing things as they are and accessing your inner wisdom?

DAY 26

Authenticity

Authenticity is a state of consciousness. We cultivate authenticity when we are not afraid to be ourselves and embrace our own experience. This often requires that we heal our childhood trauma and the reverse the patterns of self-betrayal that arise from it. Having the courage to be ourselves means that we see and accept our talents and gifts, even though they may not have been seen or encouraged by parents and other authority figures. It means that we learn to believe in ourselves and trust in our own guidance. In order to manifest our unique inner blueprint, we often must risk rejection from others who don't really see or understand who we are.

OPPOSITE STATES OF CONSCIOUSNESS: Self-Betrayal, Search for approval from parents, siblings, teachers, or peers. A strong need to fit in and be accepted by others leads to a pattern of showing up to meet their needs at the expense of our own, or to the opposite pattern of withdrawing from others so that we won't experience rejection.

THE TEACHING

In Shakespeare's *Hamlet,* Polonius says to his son Laertes: "To thine own self be true. And it must follow, as the night the day, Thou canst not then be false to any man." This was, of course, very wise advice, but it is easier said than done. Being true to ourselves requires that we individuate and free ourselves from other people's ideas of who we are and what we should do with our lives. To be ourselves, we have to detach from our parents' expectations of us and learn to follow our own inner blueprint.

An authentic person marches to his own drumbeat. He takes the path less traveled, even if it ends in a cul de sac. He learns from his mistakes and finds his own direction. Often, he has to ignore the advice of authority figures, friends or coworkers and listen to his own guidance.

An authentic person makes his own decisions and allows others to do the same. He does not allow others to decide for him, nor does he decide for others. If he makes a mistake, he owns it. He does not blame it on someone else. He takes responsibility for what he says and what he does.

An authentic person takes the time to heal his childhood wounds. If he had too much mommy or daddy and withdrew into his shell, he learns to take baby steps out into the world. He finds substitute authority figures who encourage him to be himself and express his talents and gifts.

If he had too little mommy or daddy and he became a caretaker in order to get parental love and approval, he learns to stop taking false responsibility for others and neglecting his own needs. He stops giving his power away and learns to make his own needs a priority.

If he felt neglected as a child and became a "bad boy" or narcissist in order to get attention, he learns to respect boundaries. He sees how his need to be the center of attention pushes other people away and denies him the love he so desperately seeks.

There are many subpersonalities of the False Self that we adopt in order to survive. All of them involve some kind of self-betrayal and so all must be understood and ultimately dismantled if we are going to be ourselves. This takes years of emotional healing work. That is the price we have to pay if we want to end fear-driven patterns and step into our power and purpose as authentic human beings.

Once we become aware of the unconscious programming that is running our lives, we can no longer continue to live on cruise control. We have to put our foot on the brake and slow things down. We need to become conscious of the patterns of self-betrayal and see that they don't give us the payback we expect. In fact, they drive us further and further away from the love and acceptance we seek.

Fortunately, our soul will not permit these patterns to continue indefinitely. Sooner or later the False Self will die. If we cooperate, the dismantling of the False Self can happen little by little, as we voluntarily surrender the rigid roles and co-dependent behavior that prevent us from individuating.

If however, we do not bring our awareness to our wound-driven patterns, it is only a matter of time before Humpty Dumpty falls off the wall and smashes into thousands of pieces. We may have a psychological crisis or breakdown. Often this happens in mid-age when our children are grown, our marriages are in crisis and our work has ceased to be fulfilling.

Whether it happens gently with our cooperation, or harshly with a psychological crisis, it will happen sooner or later. The mask will come off. The shell will be broken. There will be nowhere to go to escape or to hide. Shiva will find us and rip away everything that stands between us and the True Self that needs to be born. And then the Phoenix will rise out of the ashes of the transformational fire.

We will individuate and step fully into our power and purpose. Self-Betrayal will no longer be an option, for all of the strategies of self-betrayal will have been consumed in the flames.

THE PRACTICE

Today accept your uniqueness and honor your own experience even when it is different from the experience of others. Be honest with others and true to yourself. As much as possible, refrain from trying to please others at your expense.

Today, don't be a caretaker. Let others take care of themselves. Don't be a victim and expect others to take care of you.

If you are a hermit or recluse, have the courage to come out of your cave. If you are a narcissist learn to validate yourself instead of looking to others for validation.

Today be aware of when you need to "stand out" and be the center of attention, when you try to "fit in" to be accepted, or when you need to isolate or withdraw because you don't feel that others see you the way you want to be seen.

Today, realize that some people are not going to like you. Some people are not going to accept you or agree with you. Don't take it personally. That happens for everyone. Just accept that others have a different preference, belief or experience, but that does not invalidate yours. Have the courage to be yourself and follow your heart.

Today give yourself permission to have your own experience. Don't be ashamed of who you are. Don't be afraid to ask for what you need. On the other hand, do not be invested in how other people respond to you. Let them be who they are. Let them have their own experience even when they cannot support you.

When you find validation within, you are in charge of your life. You make your own decisions and take responsibility for your thoughts, feelings, words and actions. You don't have to blame others or hold them responsible for the choices that you make. You take them off the hook. And you ask them to do the same for you.

It is hard to be authentic when you are trying to make decisions for others or allowing them to make decisions for you. This is co-dependent behavior and it leads to self-betrayal on both sides.

Today, do not give your power away and allow others to decide for you. Do not misappropriate the power of others by trying to decide for them. Today, maintain healthy boundaries. Understand and take responsibility for what belongs to you and let others own and be responsible for their stuff.

Today's practice is a simple one. Be yourself and allow others to be themselves. When you see that you are giving your power away, stop and take it back. When you see that you are interfering with others, stop and take a step back. Good boundaries will guard against trespass on both sides and affirm and respect the dignity of each person.

JOURNALING QUESTION

In what ways is it difficult for you to be yourself with other people or to allow others to be themselves with you?

DAY 27

Abundance

Abundance is a state of consciousness. We cultivate abundance when we are grateful for what we have and consume only what we need. This keeps the energy moving so that our supply constantly renews itself and we always have enough. When more resources than we need flow to us, we gladly share our bounty with others. We stay in the flow by not holding on to more resources than we can use productively and not piling up possessions. Having more toys does not make us happier. It can even undermine our happiness because we take what we have for granted and cease to value it. What we don't value, celebrate or appreciate will not prosper and grow. It will become a burden that we carry.

OPPOSITE STATES OF CONSCIOUSNESS: Lack, Scarcity, Poverty, Envy of others, Lack of appreciation for what we have, Selfishness, Stinginess, Hoarding, Not sharing our resources with others, Having too little or too much.

THE TEACHING

Contrary to what many people think having more toys does not lead to more joy. Having a barn full of antique cars that you don't drive may make you the envy of others, but it does not bring as much joy as having one car that you love, work on and drive with pleasure.

How many boats or planes or houses do you need to be happy? Maybe you think you need 5 or 10 or even more. But the real answer is "none." You don't need any of this stuff to be happy. Joy comes in the celebration and productive use of the possessions you have, even if they are few.

Jesus told us that it is easier for a camel to move through the eye of a needle than it is for a rich man to enter heaven. That is because the rich man is burdened by what he owns. He must serve it, warehouse it, maintain it, protect it. He becomes the servant of what he owns. This is true for any addiction that we have.

He also reminded us that we can't take any of this with us, so we should not store up riches on earth, where they will wither and decompose. Instead we should seek spiritual riches that create joy for ourselves and others. For these riches can be shared and will grow and prosper.

On earth, forms come and go. Each is but the

container and the container has a useful life. It may be a year or two, or it might be 20 years, but in the end the form will break down and a new form with need to be created.

The Law of Thermodynamics tells us that energy cannot be created or destroyed but it can be transferred. When the old form dies, the energy embodies in a new form. This is the extraordinary process of death and rebirth that enables growth and transformation to occur.

If we are going to live in the flow of abundance, in which there is always enough for everyone, we cannot be attached to the forms. The attachment to form creates suffering, because all forms will need to be surrendered. If we want to be rich in spirit, we must align with the energy, not with the form through which it expresses.

So for example, joy is an energy. You can feel joy in a possession that you actively and enthusiastically use, but when that possession breaks or is destroyed, you need to let it go and hold onto the joy. Find another vehicle to express your joy. There are many vehicles, many pathways to choose from.

Joy and gratitude are spiritual riches, not material ones. Expressing your joy or inspiring joy or gratitude in others is the real currency of abundance. It does not matter what the form is. You can be a basketball coach working with kids or a nurse working with cancer patients. The currency is not the job description but the energy you invest and express in your job.

Abundance comes from giving and receiving energy. So choose a form that enables your energy to express as freely and spontaneously as possible. The more energy flows in your consciousness and relationships with others the more joyful and abundant your life will be.

Lack, poverty, scarcity, happen only when you stop giving your energy freely. Then the energy slows down. It may even become fixed. That creates a blockage that must be removed for the energy to flow again. How do you remove the blockage? You open your heart, you trust, you share, you stop trying to protect or control. You open up the channel so that energy can flow again.

So if there is lack in your life, it is because you are holding on and trying to control. You are not giving love, so how can love return to you?

Don't spend your time envying the possessions of other people and feeling like an unworthy victim because you have less than they do. That is a game that you cannot win. It just traps you in fear and limitation. Instead, be happy for them and hope that what they have is bringing joy into their lives. Be happy for the success of others and you will attract success into your own life. Give what you would receive and your gift will set the energy in motion. What you send out will come around to you when the time is right.

You don't succeed by withholding love from others. So extend a helping hand when you can. Give a few words of praise or a smile. Don't underestimate your gifts but give them freely.

Don't focus on what you want and do not have. That creates scarcity and lack in your life. It reinforces your victimhood. Instead, focus on what you do have and are free to give. That creates the flow of abundance in your life.

THE PRACTICE

Today, practice being grateful for what you have. Express your appreciation to others. Share your riches, your possessions and your love. What you value, share and appreciate will prosper and grow.

Don't take what you have for granted. Don't depreciate the gift that you have been given. If and when you feel you don't have enough and need more, realize that this is a sign of that you are not valuing the gifts that have been given to you. Don't look for more. Don't focus on what is absent or missing or you will reinforce the scarcity you are experiencing in your life. Focus instead on the feeling "I have been given what I need. By expressing my gratitude and appreciation, I can grow what I have." The seed can be watered and become a thriving plant.

Don't be angry at God or the universe because he gave you only a seed. Don't waste your time envying others whose plants are fully grown. Get busy, plant the seed and water it. Tend to your garden and the harvest will come.

You are not as victim. God did not give you less than he gave to others, even if it appears that way. Learn to look through the eyes of Spirit and see that God gave you exactly what you need to realize your full potential. Even if seems that He is asking you to work a little harder than your neighbor, that too can be a gift, because it will make you stronger and more determined.

Don't focus just on the material gifts that have been given to you. You cannot take them with you. Focus instead on the spiritual gifts that have been placed in your hands and share them with others. When you do that you will see how the universe is supporting you and your faith will be renewed.

JOURNALING QUESTION

Abundance comes from giving and receiving energy. Is energy flowing from you to others, and from others to you? If not, where are the blocks?

Innocence

Innocence is a state of consciousness. We cultivate innocence when we connect to our Core Self and the Core Self in others. The Core Self is our essence. It is that existential state of being that is pure and undefiled. It is not twisted by experience for it is the state prior to experience in this world. It is the original blessing given to all beings by God, who created us in His own image. This blessing was given before wrong doing, trespass or error was possible. It is the State of Heaven or Paradise before the choice to eat from the Tree of Knowledge. It is therefore an "a priori" state, before free will or choice came into play. When we see and affirm our own innocence and that of others we are acknowledging our spiritual origin and equality.

OPPOSITE STATES OF CONSCIOUSNESS: Trespass, Fear, Shame, Guilt, Judgment, Condemnation, Crime and Punishment, Sin. This is the state of being disconnected from our Core Self and that of others. It leads to various forms of attack and defense, dehumanizing and objectifying others, imprisonment, brutality, torture, and genocide.

THE TEACHING

In our justice system we are all supposed to be considered Innocent until proven guilty. Every person is supposed to be given a chance to defend himself and prove his innocence. But the reality is quite different. Those who are poor and cannot post bail are often incarcerated before they have been convicted of crimes. At the other extreme, those who are a true danger to society are often released from prison into the community without being rehabilitated. Innocent people spend twenty or thirty years in jail for crimes they did not commit and rapists and murders walk the streets. And this is supposed to be equal justice for all!

We live in a culture of blame, shame, and punishment. We do not forgive those who trespass against us. When they go to jail, we don't give them a healthy way to atone for their crimes, make amends and get the self-understanding and the skills necessary to survive when they come back into society. We warehouse inmates; we do not rehabilitate them.

Why is that? Because we label them and objectify them. We view them as bad people who have to be punished. We think that they deserve what they get. But this is not a very practical strategy for creating safety or reducing crime. If you take an angry, reactive person and beat him, he may submit for a while, but his fear and his rage only grow. When he gets out of jail, he is a walking time bomb. Any little thing can light his fuse.

Wouldn't it make more sense to use the time when he is separated from society to address the cause of his anger and his fear? Wouldn't it make sense to give him counseling, anger management training and help him develop better communication skills? Wouldn't it make sense to give him vocational training so he could find a job when he gets out of jail?

Do we think that this person cannot really be redeemed? Do we think that he has no Core Self, no original innocence, that his guilt is final and irrevocable? If so we will write him off and feel justified in doing so, even though in the end it will only hurt us.

We need to look more deeply. If we cannot see his innocence how can we embrace our own?

Jesus asked a different question to the crowd that wanted to stone the woman who committed adultery. He asked: Who among you has not sinned? Who will throw the first stone?

The teachings of Christianity help us to find equality based on the concept that we all are sinners and therefore all of us need forgiveness. That is a helpful concept, but it does not go far enough, because it does not help us understand our essential or original innocence.

If we are willing to accept the idea that we all are guilty, can we not also explore the concept that we all were innocent once and that this innocence may be something that exists "a priori." In other words, our sins may cloud or disguise our innocence but they cannot take it away from us. No matter what we have said or done, we remain an equal son or daughter of God.

We all have a heavenly origin. Yes, even the criminal. Even Cain who murdered his brother Able.

If our original innocence cannot be taken away, then the criminal can atone for his crime. He can be forgiven and he can forgive himself. And then he is restored or returned to his Innocence. It never really left him, although for a time others may have condemned him and he may have condemned himself.

If we are all innocent, then no one can be objectified and written off. Each person is worthy of love and acceptance, even if he has trespassed against his brother. Even if he has forgotten who he really is and who his brother really is. If he can forget, he can also remember. If he can sin, he can also atone for his sin.

If we are going to create a world that is safe for all of us, we must create a culture of forgiveness and rehabilitation, where those who have attacked or abused others can accept responsibility for their transgressions and make amends and restitution. This reconnects them to their Core Self. It helps them to feel the presence of love in their lives. And with that Love comes the power of transformation.

Yes, all of us are Innocent until we are proven guilty. And even when we are proven guilty, our innocence can be restored. For we never really lost it.

None of us are perfect. All of us make mistakes. If we are not condemned for our mistakes, we can learn from them and correct them. A culture of correction and forgiveness and a culture of shame and punishment are completely different. The former upholds our Innocence so that we can return to it. The latter confirms our guilt and insures that our debts can never be repaid.

THE PRACTICE

Today, remember that you are innocent until proven guilty and so is everyone else that you meet. Give yourself and everyone else the benefit of the doubt. Refrain from judging, condemning or writing people off.

Today, remember you and your brother or sister are equal children of God. You were both created in God's image, which means that you were created Innocent. You may have said or done things that have hurt others. You may be guilty of trespasses and others may be guilty of trespassing on you. But sin or guilt is a temporary state of being off the mark. It does not result in eternal damnation. Sins can be forgiven. Mistakes can be corrected.

A life of forgiveness and correction can lead us back to the kingdom of heaven. When we atone for our sins, our sins are forgiven and our original innocence shines through. We wipe the slate clean. We start anew.

Today, use every opportunity to see your innocence and that of others. Even when mistakes are made, even when trespasses occur, do not lose sight of the truth. You are not your mistakes, nor are others theirs. You are greater than that. You are the one who learns from your mistakes and corrects your errors. You are the redeemer, not the executioner.

Today be humble and give thanks to your higher

power. What God has given cannot be taken away. Humans may try to be judge, jury and executioner, but that is their error. Be compassionate with them for they are misguided. As Jesus said to God when he was being crucified, "Forgive them for they know not what they do."

Today, do not condemn another, but understand that each person does what he has the consciousness to do at any moment in time. Most sins are sins of ignorance and omission. They are not intentional efforts to hurt or deprive others.

When trespass is intentional it comes from a deep and profound lack of love and unworthiness. It is not easily corrected or forgiven, but it is the wounded child's cry for love, and sooner or later the call must be answered.

JOURNALING QUESTIONS

When have you seen the innocence of a person you previously judged or condemned?

When have you moved through your guilt and been able to see your own innocence?

DAY 29

———

Grace

Grace is a state of consciousness. We cultivate grace when we surrender to the flow of life and no longer seek to control what happens. We put our own plans aside and let God lead; we are content to be an instrument of the divine will. Grace enables us to move easily and elegantly in the direction that is for our highest good and the highest good of all.

OPPOSITE STATES OF CONSCIOUSNESS: Awkwardness, Interfering in the flow of life, Ego-agendas based on fear and lack of trust. Getting in the way, Trying to manipulate or control, Resisting or complaining about what happens, Lack of faith in and surrender to a higher power, Swimming against the tide or floundering in life like a fish out of water.

THE TEACHING

Grace only comes into our lives when we are able to surrender to what is, when we are able to know and trust that everything comes from God. Then we can stop resisting and complaining about what comes up in our lives, but instead we can submit to it and allow its purpose to reveal itself. We understand that God does not give us questionable gifts. He does not ask us to do things that we are incapable of doing. He may ask us to learn a lesson or master a skill, but as long as we are willing we are able to fulfill his request.

When we have fulfilled some aspect of God's plan, we can look back in wonder. The results are often surprising; sometimes they are even miraculous. And it becomes clear that if we were not willing to show up and do our part, the chain of grace could have been broken.

I have said many times before that we are the hands of God. He uses us to reach into the world and bring help, hope and healing to our brothers and sisters. Without us, without our reverence for life and our attunement to the divine will, hope, healing and support would not come into this world.

We are the bringers of love, not just to ourselves, but to all who share our lives. When we connect with love, we become the servant of God, the instrument of His will, and embodiment of His guidance and His grace. Our bodies, our hearts and our minds are filled with light and we shine brightly so that those who have lost their way can find their way back home.

Yes, our surrender and our reverence invite grace into our lives and when grace comes our lives are no longer tedious and full of hardship or striving. Our needs are met seemingly without effort. Resources come and go easily, because we have surrendered our egos. We have gotten out of the way, so that the river can flow and carry us downstream. We know that we no longer act alone. We have a constant guide and companion who makes straight the way. Our job is not to lead, but to follow.

The Lord is our Shepherd. He tells us what to do and where to go. He may not speak to us in a loud voice, but His will is known to us in our hearts and we learn to listen and to trust it. We know God is with us, walking before us or side by side. Indeed, we realize that we have never been alone. He has always been with us. We just did not know it and trust it.

What the Lord touches is hallowed. It is sacred. It is holy. It is sanctified. Everything God touches is full of light. When we become the servant of God, His light shines through us. We become transparent. We become an empty vessel to receive His love, and that love fills us up and overflows to others. Because we submit to His will, we become the Fountainhead where the thirsty drink and the unclean become clean again.

Of course, none of this is our own doing. We cannot take credit for the hope and healing that flows through us. As Jesus taught, all gifts come from God. We are merely the messenger or the servant delivering them.

When we say that someone is graceful, we are suggesting that they move effortlessly without struggle. They move in the flow. They are superbly coordinated. Each part of them is integral and connected to the whole. They move spontaneously. They do not crawl through life or walk like the weight of the universe is on their shoulders. They relax and let go of their burdens. They dance joyfully in the divine stream of life. Each movement, each gesture is ecstatic.

THE PRACTICE

Today, trust yourself and trust the universe. Realize that anything that comes into your life comes as a gift. Do not complain or resist. Accept the gift and let it reveal itself. Then put it to work in your life.

Today, realize that you are not here just to fulfill some ego agenda. Your purpose is not just to survive. It is to shine.

You are here by the grace of God and your life itself is a gift. If you were not worthy of love you would not be here. If you did not have a purpose, God would not ask anything of you.

Be glad that God is knocking on your door, even if He is testing you or asking you to learn an important lesson. If you do not learn to listen to God and talk with Him honestly, you will squander the gift that has been given to you.

Today learn to be reverent. Learn to appreciate the beauty around you and all of the opportunities that are coming to you, enabling you to grow and deepen your faith. Learn to surrender to your higher power so that you can understand and begin to fulfill your purpose here.

You can try to live your life without God, but it will be an awkward and ungainly life full of struggle and hardship. Why make that choice? Why try to manipulate and control just to survive when you can walk with Him and have the doors open and the path reveal itself step by step?

A life without God is like a fish out of water. It may flounder around before it dies but the end is certain. Today, stop the struggle. Stop the resistance. Stop complaining. Stop trying to control.

Learn to submit to something greater than you that has your highest good in mind and heart. There is a transcendent power that knows more than you know. Why not trust in that?

Today, show up the way that God wants you to. Learn what He wants you to say and to do. Take the time to commune with Him and drop your ego agenda. It will only create more suffering in your life.

Make today a day of surrender. Invite the grace of God into your life.

JOURNALING QUESTIONS

When have you let go of your need to control and let God be your shepherd and your guide?

What is your experience of grace manifesting in your life?

Harmony

Harmony is a state of consciousness. We cultivate harmony when we embrace a common vision, when we cooperate and support each other, when our thoughts, feelings, and values are reciprocal. Harmony is a resonance of the parts with each other and with the whole. In music harmony is created through chords where notes played together augment each other and progress together. When we are in harmony with each other, there is cohesion, coherence, congruence, balance, reciprocity, and symmetry in our expression.

OPPOSITE STATES OF CONSCIOUSNESS: Discord, Cacophony, Dissonance, Noise, Fragmentation, Tumult, Incoherence, Disturbance, Asymmetry, Lack of connection of the parts to each other and to the whole, Inability to support or complement each other, Conflict, Argument, Disagreement, Stalemate, Deadlock, Polarization. Individuals either complete with each other for control or go their own way. Disconnection, separation, and divorce result.

THE TEACHING

Without harmony there is little beauty in life. We are not able to work together to create a society that supports all of us. There is no fidelity to family, community, country or humanity. Without a shared vision, all that remains are self-serving thoughts, words and actions that emphasize our differences and pull us in opposing directions. This creates a kind of social deadlock where nothing positive gets done. Conflict, fighting, disagreement and distrust prevail. The center is lost. The poles wobble as they move further and further apart.

Such a society has no order or coherence. The parts do not support the whole. Individuals live in survival mode and organizations become dysfunctional. There is a tearing down of social connections and alliances that have brought safety and prosperity to all. The safety net falls apart. The elderly and the handicapped are forsaken. The rich become richer and the poor become poorer. The divide between religions and political parties widens. People are vilified, libeled, persecuted and abused so that others can stay in power. Might trumps right. People are imprisoned for speaking up. Humanistic values are trashed. Works of art and culture are destroyed.

All this comes from lack of harmony, from the inability of the individual to find equality with others and take his rightful place in a world that offers safety and dignity to all. Once the body of the republic starts fighting for its life, no president, premiere, emperor or strong man can slow the anger of the people or stop the flow of blood and tears. When the body of Christ falls apart, and children are sacrificed at the altar, no Pope can restore the integrity of the Church. As William Butler Yeats write: "Things fall apart the center cannot hold."

The challenge of course is to rebuild the center, to rediscover and consecrate the shared vision, to rally around a truth that we all can accept and fight for. When we are so far apart, so polarized, so at odds with each other, that seems a daunting task, yet that is our only hope.

The individual must make peace with his brother or sister. They must find common ground, even though there are some things they cannot agree on. It is not necessary for everyone to sing the same note. We can go up or down a third and find a supportive note. Together we can create harmony and achieve a depth and richness that none of us could achieve alone. If we learn to sing together, we will not go off to war against each other.

I have always said, let the enemies meet in the same hot tub and they will have a better chance of making peace than they do over the negotiating table. They might even go out for a beer and sing a few rowdy songs together. I think that is what Tip O'Neil and Ronald Reagan did, is it not?

Jesus came up with the radical idea that we could learn to love our enemies. Have we forgotten that?

If that is too much to ask, we can start with mutual respect. That is a baby step toward love. We cannot make peace in this world if we are unwilling to respect each other and treat each other as equals.

If we want resonance and harmony we will have to do our part to join together with others and build a chord, or a progression of chords. We will have to learn to play in the same orchestra.

A good orchestra will find a good conductor. It is only a matter of time. But even the best conductor will have a hard time turning a bad orchestra around. For now, even with elections coming, we should not focus on who will lead us out of the disorder and cacophony of the moment. We should focus on how we can create harmony in our own lives.

Top down approaches do not work, especially in a democracy. In a democracy the power has to come from the people. The people need to learn to respect each other and play together. When they find harmony, their leader will emerge.

THE PRACTICE

Today, don't be afraid to sing your own note, but listen also to the notes that others sing. See if you can create harmony. Don't go out of your way to focus on how you are different from others, or how your note is better than theirs. That will only isolate you. Instead, find common ground. Identify common needs. Develop a shared vision. Allow your note to resonate with the notes that others sing.

Harmony is achieved through cooperation and mutual support. It cannot be achieved through a solo journey. Today, please do not sing a sour note by seeking attention only for yourself. Invite others to sing with you. Be open to the contributions others can make. Find a way to discover that you are stronger and richer together than you are apart.

Today, don't try to be in charge. Don't try to be a conductor. What good is a conductor without an orchestra? Get down off your podium and pick up an oboe or a flute. Join the orchestra. Learn to play together.

Today is not about you only. It is about you as a member of a community. You have something important to contribute, but so do others. Find your equality with others so that cooperation can be built upon a foundation of mutual respect. Today is not about what you can achieve alone. Today is about what you can achieve in concert with others.

Today find harmony in your relationships. Don't polarize or take extreme positions. Find the center, the middle ground. Today, give up separate agendas, go beyond ego needs, and fixed beliefs. Find where you meet.

Rumi said: "Out beyond ideas of wrong doing and right doing, there is a field. I'll meet you there." Today, meet in that field where you are an equal with your partner, your child, your friend, your co-worker. See beyond appearances. Meet face to face. In that resonant field, there is peace and harmony. There is ecstatic union.

We spend most of our lives trying to individuate, trying to believe in ourselves and express our unique skills and talents. That is a worthy and necessary journey. But that is only one part of our purpose. We are not here just to play alone. We are here to learn to play together.

Part one is "Be yourself." How can you be anything else? You cannot be what someone else wants you to be. You cannot be defined by the needs and expectations of others You need to find your own unique path.

But part two is equally important. Part two is "Learn to play with others." Learn to join together and cooperate in common cause. Support a vision that is larger than yourself and learn to play your part with humility and sincerity.

What is your common cause today? Who are the people you are asked to cooperate with? What is the vision you share and what contribution is being asked of you?

Yes, today be yourself and sing your own note. But also be with others and learn to sing together. Learn to support and complement each other. Be a committed and passionate member of your family, your community, your country and your world.

JOURNALING QUESTIONS

When have you been able to cooperate and live in harmony with others?

When has your need to fly solo or be in charge prevented you from experiencing harmony in your interactions with others?

DAY 31

———

Stewardship

Stewardship a state of consciousness. We cultivate stewardship when we care for and responsibly manage the resources that have been entrusted to us. That means not being self-indulgent or short sighted in the way that we spend our money or our time. Gambling away last week's pay is not good stewardship. Running up huge debt on our credit cards or going on a shopping spree is not good stewardship. Good stewards are responsible for themselves and for the people who depend on them. They are also responsible for the care and protection of the community and the environment.

OPPOSITE STATES OF CONSCIOUSNESS: Exploitation of others and the environment, careless management of resources, recklessness, greed, waste, expediency, lack of responsibility, inability to pay one's debts, squandering resources that are needed by all of us, as well as the next generation, ignoring our fiduciary duties, stealing or defrauding others, preying upon the young, the elderly or others who are weak and cannot defend themselves.

THE TEACHING

Each of us is responsible for ourselves. We must start with that. We must take care of our health, work for a living if we can, pay our bills, and spend our money wisely. We must understand and provide for our physical and emotional needs so that we thrive and can be happy. If we can do that then we may be able to do the same for our family.

As the Taoist sages knew, a healthy family requires a healthy individual. A healthy community requires healthy families. A healthy country requires healthy communities. Resources must be used wisely from the bottom up. If you are not responsible in your own life, then you can undermine the health of your family and your community. Everything starts with you. Be at peace and peace begins its journey of manifestation in the world.

Prosperity begins in your own heart and mind. Walk your talk and do not make promises that you cannot keep. Do not spend money impulsively. Do not gamble or squander your resources to feed your addictions. Live a measured and moderate life.

Don't waste your time defending your honor or complaining about the actions of others. Don't be a victim. Live an empowered life. Know that your success is up to you, not to anyone else.

A good steward earns the respect and the trust of his family and his community. He creates stability and safety around him. He feeds, houses and protects his loved ones. He helps others in the community that need his assistance and his encouragement. He contributes to the greater good.

A good steward fulfills his fiduciary duties. He is accountable for his actions. He does not lie, cheat, steal or seek to defraud others. He treats others the way he wants to be treated. He lives by the golden rule.

A good steward works to ensure that his business is sound and that the organizations that serve his community are financially solid. He does his part to make sure that the needy are fed and the streets are safe.

He cares for nature and the health of the planet. He stands up against exploitation of the environment. He opposes short sighted development that is fed by corporate greed.

He holds companies responsible when they pollute the air, the water or the earth and he opposes government agencies and political parties that refuse to protect our right to clean air, clean water, and an earth that can feed our people.

A good steward understands that the pollution and the pillaging of the planet leads not just to global warming, with its terrible fires and floods, but to the extinction of many species that contribute to our long-term health and well-being. He knows that bio-diversity is necessary for our planet and engages in efforts to save endangered species.

A good steward is personally and socially responsible. He is a protector and a guardian of his loved ones, the citizens of his community, and the inhabitants of the planet. His arc of responsibility starts in his heart and reaches out through his words and actions to encircle the earth.

THE PRACTICE

Today, be responsible in your words and your actions. Take care of your own needs and the needs of your family. Let your care extend to those who are less fortunate in your community. Be an advocate for them too.

Today be a good steward. Do not squander your resources. Use them wisely. Do not create debts you cannot repay. Do not gamble or make impulsive purchases. Do not waste your time and your energy. Do not overconsume, take more than you need, or feed your addictions. Be moderate. Be proportional. Be measured. Make good, sustainable choices that support your well-being and that of others.

Today, care for the earth on which you live. Recycle, repair what you can so that you do not have to trash it and replace it with new products. Try not to support the throw away culture that pollutes the air and the water and contaminates the earth on which you live.

Today, give a gift to a stranger in need. Assist someone out who needs a helping hand or a little support and encouragement. Help to create safety and stability in your family and your community.

If you get confused or stressed out, take a stroll in the park. Walk by the river or on the beach. Climb a mountain path to a beautiful vista. Experience the beauty of the waters, the sky and the trees. Sit on a rock and get quiet. Take a moment to pray for the good of all the people who share your life. Let yourself by calmed and renewed by nature and remember that without her, life would wither and die.

Today be a friend to Mother Earth and all her people. Celebrate her beauty around you and do everything you can to protect and sustain it. Today, do what you can to conserve her resources so that you can pass them on intact to the next generation.

JOURNALING QUESTIONS

Are you taking good care of the resources that have been entrusted to you so that you can pass them on to the next generation?

If not, how can you take better care of those resources?

Spiritual Mastery Prayer
by Paul Ferrini

Father/Mother God:

Help me to feel my oneness with you
and my equality with my brothers and sisters.

Help me to recognize my judgments
and to look within for correction.

Help me to give up shame and blame
and to learn from my errors
so that I do not repeat them.

Help me to care for my body, my family,
my community and my planet.

Help me to create what is for my highest good
and for the highest good of others.

Help me to be responsible for my creations.

Help me give up victim consciousness
and realize that I am a powerful person
with many creative choices.

Help me to stand up for myself in a loving way
without attacking others or seeking to influence
the choices they need to make.

Help me offer freedom to others
so that I may receive it in return.

Help me reach out with compassion to those in pain,
in grief, under stress, or in limitation of any kind
and offer them hope and encouragement.

Allow my heart to open to them.
Allow my eyes to see beyond the behavior
that is motivated by fear and unworthiness.

May I offer to others and to myself
the unconditional love and acceptance you offer to me.

Help me to master my skills and talents
so that I may place them in your service
and fulfill my purpose here.

Help me to step into the role you would have me play
in inspiring, empowering and uplifting others.

Help me to trust my gifts and give them
without expectation of return
whenever the opportunity arises.

Help me to give freely and love freely
surrendering the outcome to you.

Help me surrender the need to control
so that I can live spontaneously
and with your grace.

Help me to understand and heal my wounds
so that I don't push love away
or block its presence in my heart
and in my relationships.

Help me soften and become vulnerable.
Help me learn to ask for help
and trust the help that you offer me.

Allow me to heal the past
so that I can enter the present fully.

Allow me to become a doorway
for the healing of others
and let me walk courageously through the door
that has been opened for me.

Help me surrender what is false
and establish in what is true
firmly and with conviction.

Help me to walk my talk, listen deeply,
and speak only when I have something helpful to say.

Help me to understand that the Friend
is always with me
and my only purpose is to be a Friend to others.

Help me detach from name and fame
and all forms of external authority
so that I can be guided by the authority within.

Allow me to know at all times and in all places
that the highest good of others
is and will always be my highest good.

Let all that separates me from others fall away
so that I may recognize the One Self in all beings.

Allow me to complete my work on earth
with care and humility
and return to you when my work here is done.

May all veils and barriers that separate us dissolve
so that I may dwell fully and completely
in the heart of your love.

Amen

Epilogue

Now that you have completed the 31 Days of Spiritual Awakening, you will have a better sense of how these practices can be integrated into your life. Feel free to repeat the 31 day process as often as you find it to be helpful. Repeated practice will help you master the teachings that were most difficult for you the first time around.

On some days you may wonder what the teaching and practice has to do with your life. That's okay. Each teaching represents a spiritual virtue or state of consciousness that can be cultivated through practice. In that sense, all are necessary, but some will be more relevant than others at any given time in your life.

It takes only about 15 minutes per day to read through the teaching for the day and keep it in mind as the day unfolds. This can become an important daily ritual that helps you center and connect with your Core Self. In addition, the repetitive nature of the teachings and practices insures that you will encounter them at deeper and deeper levels, even if you don't expect that to happen.

If you tire of the practice, put it aside for a while and come back to it when you feel it might be helpful. The nice thing is that on any given day when you feel that you need to have a spiritual focus, you can read the teaching and practice for that day.

DAILY VS. WEEKLY PRACTICE

Some of you may feel that a day is too short a period of time to do justice to the teachings and practices in this book. If that is the case, take a week for each one of these teachings and practices and make it a 31-week retreat. The weekly structure also lends itself to group classes and discussions. The teacher or facilitator can present the teaching and practice for the week and then the participants can work on their own and focus on the teaching and practice every day during the week. At the next meeting, people can share their experiences, further discussion can take place, and then the teaching and practice for the following week can be presented.

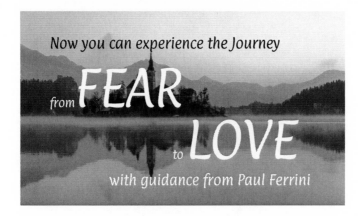

Now you can experience the Journey

from **FEAR**

to **LOVE**

with guidance from Paul Ferrini

31 SPIRITUAL TEACHINGS ON VIDEO

Paul's online course "Journey from Fear to Love" contains the complete text of this book, as well as videos of all of Paul's talks on the teachings and practices in this book. These talks were recorded at Paul's 2018 retreat in Vermont and capture the energy at the retreat.

Now, to encourage you to go deeper in experiencing this material, we are offering you (or someone you know) the entire online course with video instruction for 50% off the regular price. So instead of paying $299, the regular retail price, you pay just $149.

You will also have the option to download the video only version for $99 or the audio-only version for $27.

To take advantage of any of these options, please go to **www.lightforthesoul.com/journey-offer** and click on the link to purchase the product of your choice.

Paul Ferrini is the author of 50 books on love, healing and forgiveness. His unique blend of spirituality and psychology goes beyond self-help and recovery into the heart of healing. His conferences, retreats, and *Affinity Group Process* have helped thousands of people deepen their practice of forgiveness and open their hearts to the divine presence in themselves and others.

For more information on Paul Ferrini's work, visit his website at www.paulferrini.com or www.lightforthesoul.com. The website has many excerpts from Paul's books, as well as information on his workshops and retreats. Be sure to request Paul's email newsletter, his daily wisdom message, as well as a free catalog of his books, audio and video products.

Recent Book Titles

Light for the Soul: Daily Messages of Spiritual Awakening (Available only as Ebook)

Answering the Call of the Soul: How Suffering Transforms our Consciousness

Having the Time of Your Life: Working with Cycles to Realize Your full Potential

Healing Your Life: Bringing Love, Power and Purpose into Your Life

The Keys to the Kingdom: 8 Spiritual Practices that can Transform Your Life

The Gospel According to Jesus: A New Testament for our Time

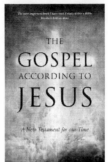

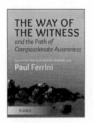   

Recent Video Products

The Way of the Witness and the Path of Compassionate
   Awareness (5.5 hours) DVDs or downloads

Healing Your Life: 12 Steps to Psychological and Spiritual
   Transformation (11 hours) DVDs or downloads

Healing Your Life Highlights (3 hours)
   DVDs or downloads

The Father Comes out of the Mother from May, 2018
   Retreat in Germany Downloads only

Creating Healthy Boundaries from October, 2017 Retreat
   in Corolla, NC Downloads only

The Keys to the Kingdom with German Translation May,
   2017 German Retreat Downloads only

Online Classes
with Text and Videos Included

Journey from Fear to Love: 31 Talks from October, 2018
   Vermont Retreat

Healing Your Life: Ferrini Teaching all 12 Steps of the
   Roadmap to Transformation

The Keys to the Kingdom: 8 Spiritual Practices that Can
   Transform Your Life

Having the Time of Your Life: Working with Cycles to Realize Your Full Potential

Opening Your Heart and Connecting to Love's Presence

Following Your Heart: The Path to Self-Actualization

Creating a Spiritual Relationship

How to Facilitate an Affinity Group

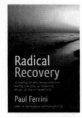   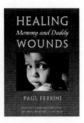

Recent Audio Products
Compact Discs and Downloads available

Healing Your Life: 12 Steps to Psychological and Spiritual Transformation—11 CD Set

The Way of the Witness and the Path of Compassionate Awareness—6 CD Set

Resurrecting Our Pain into Light: Healing Trauma, Overcoming Guilt—5 CD Set

The Keys to the Kingdom: 8 Spiritual Practices—Talks on Palm Island—5 CD Set

We are the Bringers of Love: Reparenting the Wounded Child—4 CD Set

Radical Recovery: Overcoming Addictions & Healing Your Pain—2 CD Set

Healing Mommy and Daddy Wounds—1 CD

www.lightforthesoul.com
www.paulferrini.com

Please visit the website for information on all of
Paul Ferrini's books, audio/video products, online courses,
workshops and spiritual retreats.

You can also email us at **orders@lightforthesoul.com**
or call us at **941-776-8001**

Made in United States
North Haven, CT
14 March 2024